The Gospel-Centered Woman

by Wendy Alsup

The Gospel-Centered Woman

Copyright © 2012 by Wendy Horger Alsup

First printing 2012

Printed in the United States of America

Unless otherwise indicated, Scripture quotations are from *The Holy Bible, English Standard Version*®, copyright © 2001 by Crossway Bibles, a publishing ministry of Good News Publishers. Used by permission. All rights reserved.

Scripture references marked NIV are from *The Holy Bible: New International Version*®, copyright © 1973, 1978, 1984 by International Bible Society. Used by permission of Zondervan Publishing House. All rights reserved.

The "NIV" and "New International Version" trademarks are registered in the United States Patent and Trademark Office by International Bible Society. Use of either trademark requires the permission of International Bible Society.

Scripture quotations marked NASB are from *The New American Standard Bible*®, copyright © The Lockman Foundation 1960, 1962, 1963, 1968, 1971, 1972, 1973, 1975, 1977, 1995. Used by permission.

Scripture quotations marked AMP are from *The Amplified Bible*®, copyright © The Lockman Foundation 1954, 1958, 1962, 1964, 1965, 1987. Used by permission.

Scripture quotations marked KJV are from the *King James Version* of the Bible.

All emphases in Scripture quotations have been added by the author.

All Hebrew definitions are from the Brown, Driver, Briggs, Gesenius Lexicon; which is keyed to the "Theological Word Book of the Old Testament" and accessed at www.biblestudytools.com. These files are public domain.

All Greek definitions are from a lexicon based on Thayer's and Smith's Bible Dictionary plus others; this is keyed to the large Kittel and the "Theological Dictionary of the New Testament," accessed at www.biblestudytools.com. These files are public domain.

Edited by Kathleen Firstenberg.

Special thanks to the women at Grace Church Seattle for allowing me to work through this topic with them and for being examples in action of these truths to me.

Contents

Introduction

At the first women's retreat I attended at my current church home, I met ladies I had never known before and continued conversations with others that I only casually knew. At some point in the weekend, casual conversations changed to something deeper. Women that I thought I already knew began to reveal circumstances that had seriously complicated their lives. The church leader's wife whose husband had struggled with homosexuality. The Sunday School teacher whose mother took her own life the year before. The trim, well groomed, single career woman whose brother and best friend died in a car accident when she was eighteen. The church secretary who was fired from her position at another church after complaining of sexual harassment from the pastor. The single forty something whose parents living in the same town never invited her to their home. It dawned on me over time that even though the women walking around the retreat all looked relatively well adjusted, the vast majority of them had dealt with or were currently dealing with serious trial and struggle. Something had invaded the boundaries of their lives, decimating their naïve notions of how their lives would play out. A brother dies. A mother commits suicide. A pastor betrays. A husband walks away. A boyfriend stops returning calls. Parents abandon. Miscarriage robs, and the pregnancy test never shows two lines again.

Conservative Christians, of which I am one, are famous for holding up idealistic standards as the norm toward which we should strive, especially when it comes to the good Christian woman. Depending on your circles, she may be the homeschooling, home-birthing mom who breastfed her children until pregnant with the next. Great cook that she is, she loves and serves her husband and children graciously. But even the women who meet that standard outwardly still bear the scars of depravity. I think of one friend I know who by every outward standard has it completely together. Her house is perfect, her children read years ahead of their grade level, and her Facebook updates are filled with healthy recipes she is cooking from scratch for her family. But look slightly below the surface, and you see the sexual dysfunction she experienced with her estranged father and stepmother growing up. The only responsible guardian in her life died unexpectedly when she was a struggling teenager. Another friend, a mom with a large brood of kids, also seems to fit the stereotype from the outside, but if you dig a little deeper, you see her debilitating struggle with postpartum depression. They may seem to have it together by some external standard, but that is a chimera distracting from the very serious battle between the effects of the fall in their lives and the good news of all that Christ's sacrifice on the cross has purchased for them in the way of healing. Every woman who knows Christ, single, married, with kids, or without, lives in this tension.

There is something in the gospel that meets wounded women in their brokenness. Scripture certainly gives general comfort that transcends gender. Men and women find healing from their wounds in the gospel. But there is also a particular balm to women that meets us in the woundings tied specifically to our gender. For some of us, our pain and struggles are tied to our own failures. We have sought to find our identity in something

God has not declared good and then we are frustrated when it does not satisfy. But for many more, our woundings are tied to wanting exactly what God has instructed us to want. Loving our brother, mother, or father is a good thing. Desiring marriage to a godly man and raising children for the Lord is consistent with God's earliest designs for man and woman. Submitting to a church elder fits with God's design for church authority. Confronting them for their sexual harassment fits as well. Yet many women's greatest struggles, fears, and woundings stem from their vulnerability over the very things that God has declared good for them and His specific commands to them in light of those purposes. We need to know what God declares good for His daughters, and there seem to be many Christian books to women that teach these things. But women also need to understand how the gospel equips them to deal with the vast gulf between what God declares to be His good plan for them and the reality of their daily lives. Books that address that topic are harder to find, which is the foundational purpose for this text.

When the light of the gospel shines on Scripture's teaching on the role of women in the church, the home, and life in general, it should resonate as well with the single woman watching her biological clock ticking away without a date in ten years as the wife and mom who runs her home like the virtuous wife of Proverbs 31. No one can argue that the Proverbs 31 wife is not a wonderful ideal for Christian wives. But she is an unattainable standard for many women who long for a husband and children who will rise up and call them blessed yet are powerless to attain either on their own. It is the gospel alone that equips us to bridge the gap between God's good plan for His daughters and the fallen reality in which we all live.

In this text, I want to present both God's good plan for His daughters and His grace that equips us to live in the reality where His ideals are not yet realized. God says it is not good for man to be alone. Yet there are many godly men and women who will spend their lives essentially alone. God says children are a blessing from the Lord. Yet many women who long to be mothers who raise their children for the Lord will never take that infant home from the hospital. Even for the women who do marry and raise children for the Lord, every turn in the road of life is complicated by the fall of man and the effects of depravity on our choices, our spouse's choices, and our children's choices, not to mention the depraved influences projected onto them despite our best efforts to protect them from such. Sister in Christ, the Scriptures meet us in this reality.

In the coming chapters, we will first examine what God created His daughters to be. Then we will deal with the painful truth of the ways the fall of man, including the depravity without us as well as the depravity within us, has marred the image of God He created us to bear. As hard as it is to read, it is important that we understand what is wrong with us. However, we never want to read of depravity without also holding tightly to God's good plan to redeem all that was taken by the fall. We will spend much time looking at how the gospel equips us to redeem what was lost in the fall of man. Gospel grace is meaningless without a proper understanding of the truth of our condition apart from God. But that truth will kill you without constantly bathing it in the beauty of gospel grace.

After getting this gospel foundation, we will look at various Scriptures written to women through the lens it provides. Some of these words to women are hard to read. Christ says in

Matthew 11:29 for us to take His yoke on ourselves. Over the years, the yoke has come to symbolize oppression, and there is a sense in which Christ's invitation to both men and women is very much about giving up our rights. Yet Christ is also able to say in the next verse that His yoke is easy, and His burden is light. Only the gospel can give us the proper perspective to understand how we can both give up our rights and find it a light, easy burden to bear. This is not the the same yoke of oppression by some men that Genesis 3:16 predicts and that the history of the world has proven against women. No, the yoke we carry in Christ is distinctly different as He bears it with and for us. I hope you will persevere with me through some of the hard words Scripture says to women. Believe in faith that Christ's yoke, though truly a yoke, is a burden that you can bear and, with Christ's help, actually find a light, easy burden that frees us from the much more oppressive weight of depravity.

> Matthew 11 [28] Come to me, all who labor and are heavy laden, and I will give you rest. [29] Take my yoke upon you, and learn from me, for I am gentle and lowly in heart, and you will find rest for your souls. [30] For my yoke is easy, and my burden is light."

Reflections

Section 1
Created in God's Image

Before we can discuss any other Scripture addressing women, we must first answer the foundational question, what did God create His daughters in perfection to be? This is the same question we need to answer for all believers. Husband, wife, child, sister, brother, mother, father, and friend—the answer for all believers is that we were created to be image bearers of God.

> Genesis 1 [26] Then God said, "Let us make man in our image, in our likeness, and let them rule over the fish of the sea and the birds of the air, over the livestock, over all the earth, and over all the creatures that move along the ground."
>
> [27] So God created man in his own image, in the image of God he created him; male and female he created them.
>
> [28] God blessed them and said to them, "Be fruitful and increase in number; fill the earth and subdue it. Rule over the fish of the sea and the birds of the air and over every living creature that moves on the ground."

In some Christian circles, teachers focus on wives reflecting the church and husbands reflecting Christ from Ephesians 5 to the degree that they forget every woman's identity first as an image bearer of God, marred by the fall but redeemed through the cross. Both man and woman emerge on the scene of creation foremost as image bearers of God. They are then tasked together by God with being fruitful, filling the earth, subduing it, and ruling over it. They are joint bearers of this weighty instruction, and every other instruction in Scripture to both men and women fundamentally flows from God's purposes in this moment.

One of the saddest statements I have heard a Christian woman say is that she did not feel that Jesus' example in the Gospels had anything to offer her. Jesus was a man, and she was a woman. How could He relate to her? I recently read an excerpt from a book in which the female author spoke of finding her all-time greatest inspiration as a woman from the story of Ruth in Scripture, and I was similarly bothered by her statement. I am a woman. Jesus is a man. Does this disqualify me from looking to Him first for my identity and inspiration? Not according to Scripture.

> Philippians 2 [5] Have this mind among yourselves, which is yours in Christ Jesus, [6] who, though he was in the form of God, did not count equality with God a thing to be grasped, [7] but emptied himself, by taking the form of a servant, being born in the likeness of men.

> Romans 8 [29] For those God foreknew he also predestined to be conformed to the image of his Son, that he might be the firstborn among many brothers and sisters. NIV

Paul says in Philippians 2 that our attitude should be the same as that of Christ Jesus. He says in Romans 8 that God predestined us all to be conformed to the image of His son. And the wording of Genesis 1:27 indicates that He created both male and female in His image.

I encourage any woman reading this to be careful of the priority you give the women of Scripture as examples to you in relation to your first example, Jesus. I love Ruth, Mary of Bethany, and Esther, and I am particularly intrigued by Abigail, Lydia, and Phoebe. But they must all take a backseat in terms of role models. They are valuable to us because we need a plurality of saints, male and female, who are examples of Christlikeness in a variety of circumstances. But remember also that we were not created to be like Ruth. We were created in the image of God and are being conformed back to the example of Christ. Ruth is not the ideal for women—Jesus is. Our identity is completely tied to who Jesus is and what He has done for us. He is the vine, and we are the branches. Apart from Him, we can do nothing.[1]

Whether we are struggling with PMS, nasty coworkers, a wayward husband, pregnancy fatigue, or disobedient children, Jesus is our example. His temptations, though distinct from ours in many ways, still enable Him to carry us through ours. He was tempted in every way like us. He sympathizes with our weaknesses and is fully able to equip us to deal with every struggle we face, even hormonally induced, feminine ones.

The gospels are an especially deep well from which to drink for inspiration and example as a wife, mom, sister, daughter, or friend. May we always as sisters in Christ encourage each other to look to Jesus as our first example. From that foundation, we can thank God for Ruth and the Proverbs 31 wife for how each points us to God and encourages us to be like Him.

> Hebrews 4 [15] For we do not have a high priest who is unable to sympathize with our weaknesses, but one who in every respect has been tempted as we are, yet without sin. [16] Let us then with confidence draw near to the throne of grace, that we may receive mercy and find grace to help in time of need.

---

1 John 15:5

Reflections

Chapter 1
God is Our Help

After Genesis 1 gives us the general creation of both male and female, Genesis 2 then zooms in on the creation of the first woman, giving us greater insight into the woman in particular as an image bearer of God.

Genesis 2 [18] The LORD God said, "It is not good for the man to be alone. I will make a helper suitable for him."

Some use this verse to set up marriage as the ultimate goal for every man and woman. However, our understanding of this first sinless perfection is informed by glimpses of the second. In Luke 20 Jesus is clear that in heaven we do not marry. Actually, we do marry, but Jesus is the groom. The ultimate goal in perfection for men and women is not marriage to each other. But it is relationship. What is clear in Genesis 2:18 is that it is not good for man to be alone and isolated. Man made in the image of God needed others. Married or single, we do too. God created us for community with both Him and others.

This first woman, created in the image of God, was designed and gifted particularly to be a helper suitable for Adam. The Hebrew term for helper is *ezer*, and Scripture's use of this term gives great insight into what God means when He uses the word. If you do not know God, His names, and His character, then hearing that woman was created to be some man's helper likely sounds condescending. "I'm called to be Help?! That sounds like an 18th century plantation snob referring to his servants. I'm not the Help!" Instead, if we let Scripture, not our culture, be our guide, we will see something altogether different. The Hebrew word *ezer* means to help, nourish, sustain, or strengthen. *Ezer* is used twenty-one times in the Old Testament, sixteen of which are descriptions of God himself, reflecting the fact that the woman was created to bear the image of God. Consider the use of *ezer* in Deuteronomy 33:29.

> Blessed are you, O Israel! Who is like you, a people saved by the LORD ? He is your shield and *helper* and your glorious sword. Your enemies will cower before you, and you will trample down their high places. NIV

God himself is called our helper, our *ezer*, the same word used of the first woman in Genesis 2:18. In the New Testament, the Holy Spirit is also called our Helper, Counselor, and Comforter (depending on which translation of the Bible you use. These are all translations of the Holy Spirit's role of *paraklete*, or one who comes alongside in aid). God is our Help. The Holy Spirit is our Helper. When we understand God's role as *ezer*, it gives us needed perspective. God, Sovereign Lord of the Universe, is our helper, and we, as women, are created in His image. If we hold on to the attitude that being a helper as God uses the word is condescending and substandard, we mock the name of God and His character. The role of helper is one He willingly embraces.

> Hebrews 13 ⁶So we can confidently say, "The Lord is my helper; I will not fear; what can man do to me?"

Christ says in Matthew 10:25 that it is enough for the disciple to be as his master and the servant as his Lord. It is enough that we seek to be like Him.

Consider God's example on this issue of help. In Exodus 18:4, God our help "delivered … from the sword," defending His own in contrast to attacking or ignoring the fight altogether. In Psalm 10:14, God our help sees and cares for the oppressed. Rather than being indifferent or unconcerned, He is the "helper of the fatherless." In Psalm 20:2 and 33:20, God our help supports, shields and protects. In Psalm 70:5, God our help delivers from distress. In Psalm 72:12-14, God our help rescues the poor, weak, and needy.[2]

God Himself is our example on what it means to be a helper suitable to the needs of our male counterpart, and His example reveals a high and worthy calling for women to embrace. Christian women are not glorified maids, butlers, or cooks waiting on an order to perform for a master. This is not God's example of help at all! We are called to show compassion, to support, defend and protect those in our care, to deliver from distress and to comfort. We are called to be conduits of God's grace in our homes. We are called to be like Christ.

There is much teaching now on strong male leadership in the church and home. If effort is not made in a book or sermon to carefully parse the doctrine of sanctification, we miss the differences in the image of God to which we are being conformed and the realities of our depravity until we are glorified. A woman can become very discouraged by the nebulous image of Joe Christian Dude, pastor dad, leading his family from a position of strength and power, constant in character in the marathon Christian walk. The truth is that caricature of the overcoming

---

2   Thanks to Susan Hunt and Ligon Duncan for first exposing me to this truth in their book Women's Ministry in the Local Church.

Christian man is just that ... a caricature. He doesn't exist. Or actually he does exist, but only in one single person, the perfect man Christ Jesus. For all other men, he may be the goal, but he is not the reality. Get that, ladies—even the pastors who seem like that guy, the ones that you secretly wish you'd married, do not have it together like that. Godly men may be somewhere along that journey, but none of them has arrived.

Every wife in God's service will at some point have to support a wounded husband. Do not despair over respecting, submitting to, or helping a wounded husband. Do not think that God's instructions only work for wives of Joe Pastor Dad who has it all together. If your husband is struggling, it is for this very moment that God intended you to come alongside in quiet strength to support, uphold, and encourage (often without words). If your husband is hurting, this is the time God has prepared for you. Be an *ezer* to him—helping him, sustaining him, strengthening him, and nourishing him as God does for you.

Note that Genesis 2:18 occurs before the fall. This is important because the woman was created not as a response to man's sinfulness but to his loneliness and incompleteness. All of God's creation up to that point was very good. Man being alone was the first thing that God noticed that was not good. Man was not complete. It was not good that he be alone. In order to make His creation good, God created the woman to correspond to and complement that which was lacking in the man.

Discussing the creation of the first woman as a helper to her husband can be painful and confusing if you are single, widowed, or divorced. Yet, you too are God's strong helper though you do not have a particular man toward whom to direct it. Throughout Scripture, women helped in the strongest sense of the word.

Ruth helped Naomi. Mary and Martha helped Jesus. Phoebe helped Paul. Lois and Eunice helped Timothy. Yet, I do not trivialize the reality in which you find yourself. As God said in the garden and you well know by your own life experience, it is not good for man (or woman) to be alone. We all need relationship. Thankfully, we are given great spiritual examples of singleness in the Bible. The example of Paul (and Jesus!) teaches us the profound kingdom value of the life of a single man or woman fully committed to God.

Ruth is a particularly compelling female example. Her story is well known because of her marriage to Boaz that resulted in her bearing a son in the lineage of Christ. But the most compelling aspects of her character were forged and exhibited when she was a widow with few prospects for marriage. Long before Boaz entered the picture, she was a strong helper in every God-inspired sense of the term to those God had called her to love and serve.

The gospel of Christ meets us in all of these realities. Single woman who longs for relationship. Married woman who longs to have a husband who loves her as Christ loves the church. Divorced woman whose marriage ended in betrayal. Widow who feels the hole in her heart daily. The truth for all of us is that the fall of man has marred the image of God in us. We are not what He created us to be. The fall of man has also marred the environment in which we live. Others around us are not what He created them to be. Loved ones betray. Loved ones die. And sometimes, loved ones simply never show up.

In Christ, we start to see the reclamation of God's image in us through redemption. In Ephesians 1 and 2, the Apostle Paul lays out for us all Christ's death on the cross has accomplished for us. He expounds on it more in Ephesians 3 and 4. Then he opens Ephesians 5 with the amazing phrase, "Therefore be imitators of God." Finally, we have the tool for bridging the vast gulf between our created image in Genesis 2 and the fall of Genesis 3. Now, in Christ, we start to reclaim His image in us, and Paul in Ephesians 5 and 6 fleshes out what this looks like across the board—husband, wife, parent, child, coworker, boss, and general relationships with the church.

We will begin to unpack this gospel in the next section. However, before that, we need to first consider the negative results of the fall of man. It may be tough to read, yet hope is coming. Please persevere with me through a discussion of the very real problem the fall of man ushered in for women.

Reflections

Chapter 2
The Fall of Man and Woman

What is wrong with me?! The answer to that question is complicated. I have my particular, personal shortcomings and struggles, and they are likely very different than yours. But I also share a global problem with others of my gender. The painful truth is that the fall of man has marred the image of God He created us as women to bear. It marred the image of God in men as well, but in this chapter, I want to examine the fall of man and its implications for women in particular. However, we never want to talk of the effects of the fall and human depravity without also holding tightly to God's good plan to redeem all that was lost. Gospel grace is meaningless without a proper understanding of the problem—the truth of our condition apart from God. But that truth will kill you and me without constantly bathing it in the beauty of gospel grace. Though it may be painful to examine, we will miss the incredible answer the gospel provides if we misunderstand or minimize the very real problem Scripture foresees as a result of the fall for women.

> Genesis 3
> [16]To the woman He said,
> "I will greatly multiply
> Your pain in childbirth,
> In pain you will bring forth children;
> Yet your desire will be for your husband,
> And he will rule over you."

Consider this major outcome of the fall in the life of the woman—her desire will be for her husband. This desire is couched between two painful things, childbirth and oppression.[3] Apart from modern medical intervention, no one would deny that childbirth remains today very painful for women. How a woman interprets that pain and responds to it seems strongly influenced by her culture or upbringing. I grew up in a family and culture that did not think deeply about the theological beginnings of the pain of childbirth. Most in my family chose medical intervention as needed to minimize pain. Some women I know have strong feelings about natural birth. Among my friends, their concern is mostly over unnecessary medical intervention rather than the theological implications of the fall.

Outside of westernized culture, divergent views become more visible. One doula working in the Middle East shared with me how doctors from one country were perceived as choosing C-sections because they were compassionate and did not want women to suffer pain in childbirth. Midwives from another country were perceived as wanting women to suffer a little bit at first because they thought that was what women were supposed to do. In many cultures, childbirth is a rite of passage for women. From an early age, they are raised with the assumption that they will begin bearing children at a very young age. Childbirth is associated in those cultures with the grieving of the passing of their innocence and childhood. Women may wail during labor much like professional mourners in the Bible. Regardless of cultural background, what is clear is that childbirth is painful, even with modern medical intervention.

---

3   Rule in Genesis 3:16 is not a term for the kind of grace-filled leadership that Ephesians 5 describes. The term *rule* indicates oppression.

It is also clear that men still rule over women in oppressive ways, though great advances in women's rights have been made in western cultures over the last hundred years. Western culture accounts for only around 10% of the world's population. In Saudi Arabia, women still do not have the right to vote and must be accompanied by a male guardian in public.[4] In China, there were 19,000,000 more boys than girls under the age of fifteen in the last census due to sex selective abortions.[5] Even with gains in many cultures, men still rule over women in oppressive ways in most of the world. Despite it all, as the Bible predicts in Genesis 3:16, women desire men.

What does the Bible mean when it says the woman will desire the man? The Hebrew word for desire is used only two other times in the Old Testament.

> Genesis 4 [7] If you do well, will you not be accepted? And if you do not do well, sin is crouching at the door. Its desire is for you, but you must rule over it."

> Song of Solomon 7 [10] I am my beloved's, and his desire is for me.

There are several historic interpretations of the phrase "your desire will be for your husband" from Genesis 3:16. Some believed it represented a sexual desire. However, its use in Genesis 4:7 seems to contradict that meaning of the word. Others in the history of the church believed it meant simply desire, craving, or strong longing. That meaning fits all three uses. Different authors of different books in the Bible will

---

4   Women are scheduled to gain the right to vote in Saudi Arabia in 2015.
5   Baculinao, Eric. (2004). China grapples with legacy of its 'missing girls." NBC News. Retrieved 10.1.2012, from http://www.msnbc.msn.com/id/5953508/ns/world_news/t/china-grapples-legacy-its-missing-girls/

sometimes use words with slightly different connotations. The author of Genesis seems to use this strong craving in unhealthy, idolatrous ways while Solomon uses it in a healthy sense. In the 1970s, some first suggested that this desire meant a woman's desire against her husband to dominate him.[6] However, while that use of the word might fit Genesis 4:7, it does not fit Song of Solomon 7:10.

The standard definition of this word for desire in Hebrew lexicons is longing or craving, which fits all three of the uses in the Old Testament. In Genesis 3:16, the phrase seems to reflect a longing bordering on idolatry for something from the man that the woman was created to receive from God alone. The issue is best understood if we make the simple substitution of God for her husband. Her desire should be for her God. Instead, her desire/craving/longing is misplaced.

Psalm 73 talks of such desire when it is correctly directed toward God. In that chapter, the Psalmist recounts his great emotional battle, which is a good summary of the overall struggle of life in a fallen world. The wicked flourish, those who follow God are mocked, and the Psalmist seems on the verge of losing his faith. Then he enters the presence of God, and the life of faith begins to make sense again. The grand climax of this psalm is found in verses 25 and 26. In his great struggle to make sense of life, here is his resolution.

> [25] Whom have I in heaven but you?
> And there is nothing on earth that I desire besides you.
> [26] My flesh and my heart may fail,
> but God is the strength of my heart and my portion forever.

---

6 Foh, Susan. What is the Woman's Desire? Westminster Theological Journal, 1974-75, 383.

When God is the object of our desire and strong longings, things start to make sense again. The Psalmist realized that God was his portion or inheritance. God was his strength. There is *nothing* on earth that can replace what only God can provide to sustain our hearts.

Genesis 3:16 gives us a picture of a woman who looks to the man in her life for emotional and spiritual affirmation and provision in ways that God alone is supposed to provide. As Augustine said, our hearts are restless until they rest in God.[7] The problem for the woman is one of idolatry, and I can bear witness to this truth. I looked to men to meet needs in my heart they could not meet on their best day—emotionally, spiritually, physically. Instead of recognizing my sovereign, compassionate, and wise Father in heaven as the place to which I should have looked, I started looking within myself once the men in my life disappointed me.

I frankly cannot imagine how women navigate this in cultures where oppression is sanctioned by the government. How do you face this need in your heart when it is compounded by utter dependence on men for physical safety and financial support in countries where you cannot even vote? In westernized cultures with greater freedoms for women, this craving is clearly evident. There is the bikini barista at the coffee stand who did not get affirmation from her father so she seeks it among unknown men in cars driving past. There is the porn star who doubles as a comedian. Driven by her desperate craving for applause or laughter, she exploits herself as the butt of her own jokes when she is not baring herself physically. Media is full of examples of women actively participating in their own

---

7   Augustine, Confessions 1:1.

exploitation out of some misplaced need for affirmation or approval.

While media exploits this need in women for affirmation, our western culture has adopted its own reactions against it. Women often perceive weakness or strength among each other by how they react when men fail them. The perceived strong feminist woman is the one who does not need men. She can do it on her own. The perceived weak woman is the one who continues to follow loser men around like a whipped puppy, the kind of woman Hollywood preys upon. In Christ, however, we have a new and different way altogether. The woman bought by Christ who is set up as God's honored daughter with full access to the King of kings has her needs met in Him. God pours into her. God equips her. God satisfies her emotional, spiritual, and physical needs. Then and only then can she let go of her perceived rights and stay engaged as the strong helper to the man that God created her to be.

Even as a believer, this misplaced desire shows up in my life. I have often grasped and clamored at the men in my life, "Lead me spiritually. Provide for me physically. Affirm me emotionally. Make me feel good about myself!" When my husband cannot do that for me to the extent for which I long, I attempt to lead myself spiritually, provide for myself physically, and seek outside affirmation for myself emotionally. Instead, I do not need to change my desire or craving. I simply need to change the object of it.

Directing such desires and longings to God blesses every woman in a way that transcends marital status or stage of life. No matter our culture or upbringing, the gospel calls us back to relationship with God as the solution to this strong longing.

We cry out, "God, I need you to meet the spiritual void in my life!" And God says, "Certainly, child. I will not leave you as an orphan. I have sent my Spirit to bring to your remembrance all I have taught you, for apart from me, you can do nothing."[8]

"God, provide for me physically!" God answers, "You can trust me, child. Do not worry for your physical needs. As I provide for the birds and flowers, I will provide for you."[9]

"God, help me emotionally!" God says, "Yes, child. Meditate on all I have declared over you through Christ. You have received the full rights of a child of the King.[10] I will receive you one day into my arms with the affirmation, 'Well done good and faithful servant.' Find joy and rest in Me."

Until we grasp our root problem, we will not fully understand how the gospel equips us to reclaim God's image in us as His daughters. Apart from Christ, our tendency after the fall is to aim our desire toward men and set them up as being able to meet needs in our lives that only God can meet, and there is no limit to how desperate a woman can become to get a man to meet that need.

I mentioned earlier that some interpret Genesis 3:16 to mean that the woman will have a desire to control or dominate her husband. Certainly, many women, myself included, have attempted to control situations in our homes through either artful manipulation or outright demands. However, such control tactics are not the manifestation of an innate desire to dominate the men in our lives. Instead, we resort to manipulation and control because we long too hard to rest in the men in our lives. When we misunderstand the root problem, our solutions

---

8   John 15
9   Matthew 5-7
10   Galatians 4:5

25

are either inadequate or downright hurtful to those we counsel.

Consider how the fall played out in the lives of some of the earliest women in Scripture compared to their creation in perfection as strong helpers. In the opening moments of the fall of man, Eve, the prototype strong helper, believed Satan's lies rather than God's truth. Instead of being the help to Adam as God intended, she encouraged him right into the fall of man.

In Genesis 15, God promised Abraham that he would be the father of a great nation. In the next chapter, his wife Sarah is barren and manipulates Abraham into getting her servant pregnant. Then, after giving her servant to Abraham and talking him into sleeping with her, Sarah gets bitter at Abraham for the whole situation. Sarah didn't trust God's promises, took matters into her own hands, nagged her husband into participating in her very bad plan, and then was bitter with him over the consequences, leaving Hagar to pay the price.

This pattern continues throughout the stories of the women of Genesis. In Genesis 27, Rebekah manipulates circumstances in her home, getting her son to trick her husband into giving his blessing to her favorite of their children. In Genesis 30, Rachel and Leah have a fertility war. Rather than looking for the ways they could help, nourish, and protect their families, they each manipulate every factor they can to see who can have the most sons. They show little trust in God's hand to provide for them. Just in case we are not convinced of the pattern, Genesis 38 gives us the story of Tamar, who manipulates her father-in-law into thinking she's a prostitute and sleeping with her so that she will have an heir. These women were not helpers in the God-inspired sense of that term. They were nagging manipulators intent on taking matters into their own hands because they did not trust God with their husbands or their situation. They each had strong desires, but again and again, they failed to see God as the sustaining object of it.

Nothing I have said to this point should be mistaken as placing the sole blame for these circumstances upon the women in these stories. Each of the men seriously abdicated their responsibilities. Judah in particular acknowledges this clearly with Tamar. But if you look at other women in Scripture such as Abigail, Esther, or Ruth, you see that women's ability as strong helpers in the image of God are not dependent on the righteousness, or even existence, of men in their lives.

The women of Genesis give us insight into the fall of man's affect on women. They twisted their role as helpers suitable for their husbands and became manipulators who sought to control circumstances out of their distrust of God. The word manipulate comes from the Latin for *hand*. It means to influence, manage, or control to one's advantage by artful, subtle, or indirect means, i.e. taking things into our own hands. Contrast this with faith. Faith is a confident belief in the truth or trustworthiness of a person, idea, plan, or thing. The first question the women of Genesis prompt me to ask myself as a believing wife is *do I trust God in my marriage*? I encourage any wife reading this to ask yourself as well. Do you have confidence in God's plan and trustworthiness? Or do you believe that to protect yourself, you have to manipulate circumstances by taking things into your own hands? Second, I am prompted to ask myself what am I looking toward to feel good about myself? To give my life meaning? And what am I willing to manipulate to make that happen?

Thankfully, the Genesis account of manipulating, non-*ezer* women is not the last word on women in Scripture. The Genesis account is not even the last word on the women of Genesis. The women with some of the harshest stories and biggest failures in Genesis are mentioned in the New Testament not in light of their notorious failures but as faithful daughters of God in the line of the Messiah.

Consider the genealogy of Jesus in Matthew 1.

> [2]Abraham was the father of Isaac, Isaac the father of Jacob, Jacob the father of Judah and his brothers,
> [3]Judah the father of Perez and Zerah, whose mother was Tamar ...

Tamar, who tricked Judah into sleeping with her in Genesis, is greatly honored by being one of only three women mentioned in the lineage of Christ.

Later, Hebrews 11, the faith chapter, says of Sarah, "By faith Sarah herself received power to conceive, even when she was past the age, since she considered him faithful who had promised."[11] The last we heard of Sarah and Tamar in Genesis was rather negative. Yet, in the New Testament, we see God honoring them as a result of His transforming plan for their lives. Sarah goes from being the woman known for manipulating her husband into sleeping with her maid to being commended for her faith in God to fulfill His promises. That is redemption! We too have the hope of God's power to transform us from women who take matters into our own hands out of distrust of God's plan and purposes into women who, in the image of God, help, strengthen, and support in our realm of influence, trusting God with the example He has given us.

Genesis reveals a lot of bad choices among women living in

---

11 Hebrews 11:11

oppressive circumstances. They had a craving and longing, just like us, for provision and affirmation. Yet again and again, they directed that longing to the wrong person or thing, with disappointing results. In your own culture and modern context, to what object do you direct your longing or craving? Where do you look when you long to feel good about yourself? To find meaning for your existence?

In the next chapters, we will flesh out God's provision for us and His affirmation over us. But for now, just hear again the Psalmist's resolution to this problem in his own heart.

Psalm 73
[25] Whom have I in heaven but you?
    And there is nothing on earth that I desire besides you.
[26] My flesh and my heart may fail,
    but God is the strength of my heart and my portion forever.

Reflections

Section 2
Redeemed to Reflect God Once More

God created us as strong helpers in His image and gave us a great example in Himself of what He meant when He used that term. Then Adam and Eve sinned, and the image of God we were created to bear was marred and distorted. Instead of looking to God to meet their cravings and longings, women often look to men to satisfy the longings in their heart that only God can satisfy. The gospel gives us the solution to this misplaced desire.

We were created in perfection, but we are now marred by the fall. Yet, even as God announced the curse in Genesis 3, He alluded to our redemption through Christ from all that was broken in the fall of man.

Genesis 3
[15]I will put enmity between you and the woman,
    and between your offspring and her offspring;
  he shall bruise your head,
    and you shall bruise his heel."

God put enmity or warfare between Satan and the woman, between his offspring and hers. When Christ came, Satan bruised his heel, but Christ dealt a knock out blow to Satan's head. Redemption is here! Yet what does that word even mean? Our lives still reflect much of the fall and curse. What has Christ done on the cross, and how does that good news equip us to live in the tension between what God created us to be and the reality of our lives in a fallen world?

I will attempt in this section to flesh out the gospel so that we can apply it as strong helpers living in a fallen world. I want to explore the meaning of the word gospel. Yet defining the gospel is a bit like defining marriage, only harder. I can give a three sentence summary of the essence of the meaning of marriage that would in no way do justice to the various parts that make up the whole of marriage in real life. So it is with the gospel.

In this section, I start to unpack the meaning of the word gospel. But in reality, you will be left with glimpses of just a few facets of the multifaceted gem which Christians for ages have called good news. Our entire lives should be spent exploring this gem and the subsequent illumination it gives all aspects of our lives.

Chapter 3
Godliness with Contentment

A few years ago, I was invited to speak at a women's conference on contentment. The topic did not inspire me, but I had learned long before the value of studying something in Scripture that did not at first resonate with me. I set off on a study of contentment, using I Timothy 6 as the starting point. After a few weeks of study, I realized that God was opening my eyes to wonderful things in His word, not just on the traditional idea of contentment but on the wonders of the gospel applied. What I was learning ministered deeply to me in the longings in my heart tied to my creation as a strong helper in the image of God. Though this section is about the gospel and redemption, I am going to discuss it by way of a short study on contentment in Scripture. This may seem a roundabout way of examining and applying the gospel, but we will clearly get there in the end.

When I started studying the topic of contentment, the first thing I had to do was unpack my biases against the term. I had baggage from my conservative Christian upbringing, in which contentment was taught as an obligation, mostly during women's devotionals. I was often left wondering, "Don't men need to learn contentment too?!" What is contentment, and what does Scripture mean when it uses the term?

1 Timothy 6 [6] But godliness with contentment is great gain, [7] for we brought nothing into the world, and we cannot take anything out of the world. [8] But if we have food and clothing, with these we will be content.

Paul says that godliness is a means of great gain when accompanied by contentment. The way he words it makes it sound like the gain of godliness is severely compromised without contentment.

Some of you reading this probably resonate with the term godliness. Some of you do not. Some reading this likely think of yourselves as content. Some do not. For many of us, at face value, the phrase *godliness with contentment* sounds far off and unattainable. Perhaps, it sounds like yet another obligation to add to the long list of obligations you already have. "Great—it's not enough just that I be godly. Now I've got to be content too?!" Is contentment an obligation? Is it something I need to do or be? What does the phrase *godliness with contentment* mean and how is it even possible?

To unpack any baggage when we read these words, we should understand what the Bible actually means when it uses these terms. First, there is the term *godliness*. Growing up in the church, I thought it meant being like God—doing God's things and responding in God's ways. I have always felt intensely the ways I am not like Him. Godliness seemed unattainable. It sounded like a far off, lofty goal.

In Scripture it is actually a simpler concept. The Greek word for godliness is *eusebia*, meaning devotion or piety. It comes from a Greek word that means dutiful. Some synonyms are respect, veneration, or awe. The opposite is irreverence.

Godliness simply means you are devoted to God. You are aligned with Him. You keep a posture toward Him. You love Him. It is the Greatest Command.[12] Most of us reading a Christian book on how the gospel informs womanhood probably

---

12 Matthew 22:36-40

generally consider ourselves devoted to God. In an honest assessment of ourselves, we love Him, which is why we care about this topic. But you can be godly—you can show reverence, piety, and devotion to God and His things, loving Him from a sincere, pure heart—without being content. The one does not imply the other. There are godly people, devoted to God, who are not content, and that is not particularly great gain according to Paul. The gain of devotion to God is severely compromised without contentment.

It makes sense to me that godliness and contentment are distinct from each other. My problem is not that they are separate, but that they seem mutually exclusive. They seem completely incompatible. There are facets of devotion and piety toward God, i. e. godliness, that seem to fundamentally war with my idea of contentment. What godly person is going to be content with this mess of a life, right?

As godly, devoted believers, we are called to pray that God's kingdom come. Yet we live in a world where we are constantly faced with all the ways His kingdom is not yet fully realized—sickness, death, suffering, and sin. It's the *already, but not yet* nature of God's kingdom on earth. The kingdom of God is at hand; in one sense it is *already* here. But there is so much *not yet* realized. Hebrews 2:8 says that everything is subject to God the Son, yet we do not see everything subject to Him at this moment.

> ... putting everything in subjection under his feet." Now in putting everything in subjection to him, he left nothing outside his control. At present, we do not yet see everything in subjection to him.

For you, where in your life is the kingdom of God not yet

fully realized? Where in your life is this disconnect between what God says is good, for which we should be longing, and your earthly reality?

Many reading this have experienced infertility or the loss of a child. You love God and desire to raise children for His glory. He himself calls them a blessing. Yet this righteous kingdom desire is unfulfilled, and you ache as you process it.

Maybe you are a wife who wants to honor God in your marriage, but your husband undermines and deflates you constantly. Your love of God draws you to raise your children to love Christ. Yet your husband is at best apathetic and often actually hostile to Christianity.

Many of you are godly single women longing for healthy relationships. You have a piety and devotion toward God yet daily experience loneliness that seems far from the perfect community for which He created you to enjoy.

Maybe you are a daughter whose parents are close to divorce. You long for them to embrace God's plan for their marriage yet daily watch two of the people you most love in this world wound and sin against each other.

The examples could go on and on. Conflict in the church. Conflict in the world. "God how do I be content in the midst of this sin? This suffering? This conflict?" It is one thing to be content with your bank account or your clothing options. But how do you reconcile godliness with contentment when your parents divorce, your church splits, your husband leaves, or your child rebels? How do you reconcile it when none of them ever show up in your life in the first place? Are we really supposed to be content in the midst of these things in our lives that do not yet reflect God's kingdom and God's goodness? Godliness and contentment seem mutually exclusive in such situations.

Now, consider the word contentment. The Greek word is *autarkeia*. It means a condition of life in which no further aid or support is needed or in which you have sufficient supplies for the needs of the moment. It is used one other place in the New Testament. There, it is translated sufficiency.

> 2 Corinthians 9 [8]And God is able to make all grace abound to you, so that having all sufficiency in all things at all times, you may abound in every good work.

Sufficiency means you have what you need. You have adequate provision and adequate supplies.

In a world of people and situations that consistently miss the mark of God's perfection and all He intended us to be as His image bearers in Eden, you and I have adequate, sufficient supplies for this season. For this struggle. We have something that bridges the gap between those things for which our piety and devotion to God calls us to long and the reality of our experience at this very moment. We have a bridge between our godly longing and our fallen reality that sufficiently equips us to deal with each struggle.

It is the gospel.

The gospel is this bridge. God has done something through the life, death, and resurrection of Christ by which He is able to make "all grace abound to you." He has done something through Christ that sufficiently equips you and me so that we are abundantly supplied for every good work He has called us to do, this kingdom living that stands in such stark contrast with our fallen earthly reality.

Gospel grace sufficiently equips you to face your parents'

divorce. Gospel grace sufficiently equips you to face unreconciled conflict between Christians. Gospel grace sufficiently equips you when your husband fails you, your children rebel, or your friend rejects you. Gospel grace sufficiently equips you in your suffering over sickness and death. It also sufficiently equips you to face your suffering over sin. It paves the way for you and me to confess our sins against others and forgive those who have sinned against us.

The gospel is the bridge to this confidence in God's sufficient supply for us in this very moment, though there is a grand void between the perfection of the Garden of Eden and the brokenness in our lives right now. However, the terms gospel, grace, gospel-centered, and grace-based are more often thrown out than accurately defined. The gospel is not a buzz word, and I do not want to use it in a careless way. So I need to flesh out what I mean when I say the answer is the gospel.

The gospel is a big concept. It encompasses all that the life, death, and resurrection of Christ accomplished for us, and this gospel changes everything. The New Testament writers borrowed the word gospel from the Roman empire. When a new emperor was crowned, the Romans won a war, or something else important happened, they would send evangelists (literally good news-ers) to tell people about the good news or gospel. When the word gospel was applied by the disciples to the life, death, and resurrection of Christ, the idea was that the world had fundamentally shifted. Things are different now.

Jesus is King. His reign has begun in the world. His Spirit has been poured out and gives the power for that reign to spread. This reign changes everything—everything within us and everything outside us. I have mentioned Hebrews 2:8 which reminds us that while He is king, we do not yet see everything subject to Him as we will one day. Jesus instructed us in the Lord's Prayer to pray that His kingdom would come. After Jesus' ascension and the giving of the Holy Spirit, Paul prays for us at the end of Ephesians 1 that our eyes would be opened to the implications of Jesus' power and authority for our lives. Jesus is king, and we can spend the rest of our lives studying the many facets of this gospel diamond and still have more to learn and explore as His reign spreads.

In terms of understanding how to be a strong helper in a fallen world, I want to focus on the technical theological ideas of justification and sanctification. You do not need to be able to define those terms to live in light of what Christ provided through His life, death, and resurrection, but the meaning behind those words helps us answer an important question. What did Christ's life and death bring to the table that empowers you and me to live confidently as strong helpers in a broken world?

My understanding of the gospel well into adulthood was anemic. I grew up in conservative churches where I learned short pithy sayings that "summed up" the gospel. I took evangelism classes so I could walk someone through the "Romans' Road." At Christian camp, I memorized a flip chart that we used to lead campers to Christ. Looking back, I realize that I could only articulate a small part of the gospel. I knew one facet of the good news of Christ and naively thought I had understood and mastered it all.

Those presentations of the gospel in my youth focused on the universal nature of our debt, that "all have sinned and come short of the glory of God," and Christ's payment of our sins on the cross.[13] They focused on the value of Christ's death for me. But they did not focus on the value of His *life*. Over the years, I have come to understand that the good news of Christ is not just that, through Jesus, my debt to God is canceled. God did more than just bring my account up to zero. He also has lavished positively His grace on me, crediting to my account Christ's righteousness.

> 2 Corinthians 5 [21]For our sake he made him to be sin who knew no sin, so that in him we might become the righteousness of God.

It is the Great Exchange. I had an infinite debt to God. I was by nature deserving of His wrath, dead in my sins and unable to save myself.[14] I have benefitted greatly from Christ's death, the penal substitution. But, oh, the benefits to me from His life, called imputed righteousness in theological circles. Christ's righteousness is in my spiritual bank account now, and that is every bit as precious as the payment for my sin.

Consider an inmate who has received a long sentence that he rightly deserves. With no hope of freeing himself, his sentence is suddenly marked, "Paid in full!" By the mercy of the judge and sacrifice of another, he walks out of jail a free man. Yet, he is broke. While he is momentarily grateful that he no longer has a debt to society, he faces a long, daunting road. He cannot buy lunch. He cannot pay a taxi to take him home (if he even has a home). If he does not have someone on the outside helping him, he cannot pay for a hotel room for the night. His best chances are to sleep under a bridge and steal food wherever he can find

---

13 Romans 3:23
14 Ephesians 2:1-3

it. He is set up for failure. He is set up to return to a life of crime. His only hope is to pull himself up from the bootstraps. But pitfalls surround him, and he has virtually no safety structure to keep him from utterly failing.

This illustrates the very great difference between a view of the gospel that ends with penal substitution and one that also strongly embraces imputed righteousness. To impute means to attribute something to someone. Christ's righteousness has been attributed to us, and the ramifications of that are precious.

Paul emphasizes this aspect of the gospel in Ephesians. He starts off with a bang in Ephesians 1. In Christ, you are blessed with *every spiritual blessing.* He then goes through those blessings in detail, praying at the end of Ephesians 1 that his readers would come to understand the wealth of this inheritance in their accounts and the greatness of the power at work on their behalf. Only then does he get into the fact in Ephesians 2 that we were dead in our sins, by nature deserving of God's wrath and alienated from God. Paul seems to understand, under the Spirit's inspiration, that we first need to know that our bank account is full and that we have resources. Just being spared death does not prepare you for life.

God has not brought us from our deficit to just dead even in our spiritual account. Christ has done much more than simply pay our debt. Now, in Christ, I have an abundant surplus in my account because God sees me wearing Christ's robe of righteousness.[15] I am righteous! And not by works of my own. God has lavished this righteousness to my account fully by His mercy and grace, and I can rest in it.

Now re-read 2 Cor. 9:8 in that context.

---

15 Isaiah 61:10

And God is able to make all grace abound to you, so that having all sufficiency in all things at all times, you may abound in every good work.

Here you are in this moment where your godliness, your devotion to God and desire for His kingdom to come, seems at war with your reality. God says in response, "No, you can rest. You are sufficiently supplied by My grace. I have blessed you with every spiritual blessing there is. You have a spiritual bank account that is full, and you are equipped with an abundance from which to draw for the good deeds I have for you as you wait on King Jesus to return in all His glory."

In Christ, I am the inmate set free from my well-deserved sentence who has the bank account and resources of a child of the king. I have resources for every spiritual need that comes my way. When I am provoked to anger, I have spiritual resources. When I am sinned against, I have spiritual resources. When I am tempted with gluttony, lust, selfishness, or gossip, I am fully equipped for battle. When my church has conflicts, I am equipped. When my parents sin, I am equipped. When my husband fails me, I am equipped. When loved ones suffer, I am equipped. When loved ones sin against me (or I against them), I am equipped. Paul says that the same power that raised Christ from the dead is the power at work in me![16]

This aspect of the gospel has radically altered my perspective on my circumstances in relation to my creation as a strong helper in the image of God. I had often wanted to help in the strongest sense of the term, but my perceived lack of emotional, spiritual, or physical reserves within myself seemed an insurmountable barrier.

---

16 Ephesians 1:18-20

Circumstances after the birth of my children put a spotlight on this perceived lack. I had two extremely energetic little boys twenty months apart. My husband's job schedule was chaotic. I walked through intense conflict between Christians and journeyed with two friends through dark depression in the midst of it. We have emerged somewhat from that season, particularly the intensity of the toddler years, but the struggle is still fresh in my mind. My husband would come home from work to find me gripping the rocking chair trying to not run crying from the room the moment he entered. Many days, I sat on the side of my bed shell shocked, thinking, "This is not what I signed up for in church youth group."

I call it the prosperity gospel of conservative evangelicals. If you make the right choices when you are young, you set yourself up for a good life, or so they teach us in youth group and Bible college. Instead, here I was well into marriage and raising my children, and my life did not feel like I expected. This was not what I thought would happen when I committed myself in youth group to following Jesus. Then I walked with friends whose struggles made my trials and burdens look like child's play.

One friend's husband just walked out. He did not come home from work one day. With no note or explanation, we thought he was dead and organized searches on foot to locate his car or body. Finally, it became clear he had just walked away. His wife, my friend, was pregnant with their third child at the time. I remember sitting across from her on the sofa in her living room praying to God in desperation, "How do I reconcile this? How are You good in this? Where is the gospel in this?" The word content sounded like sacrilege in that moment. It sounded like blasphemy. I could not tell her to be content with such circumstances. What person who loves God and longs for His kingdom could possibly be content with a husband abandoning his wife and children?!

Yet, I knew in theory there was something in Christ's life, death, and resurrection that was supposed to speak into even this. That was February. In May, my aunt was murdered after coming home from church one Sunday morning. I cannot begin to unpack here the wrestling between godliness and contentment in my heart provoked by that one act by a violent kid none of us knew. This was in conjunction with an intense conflict between Christian friends that resulted in what seemed like the exact opposite of God's kingdom coming and His will being done on earth as it is in heaven. In the midst of all this, I was writing *By His Wounds You are Healed: How the Message of Ephesians Transforms a Woman's Identity*. I was becoming intimately acquainted with Paul's presentation of these aspects of the gospel (Christ's payment of our sins and His lavish grace applied to our account) and his prayer in light of them at the end of Ephesians 1.

> [18] having the eyes of your hearts enlightened, that you may know what is the hope to which he has called you, what are the riches of his glorious inheritance in the saints, [19] and what is the immeasurable greatness of his power toward us who believe, according to the working of his great might [20] that he worked in Christ when he raised him from the dead and seated him at his right hand in the heavenly places,

That prayer became my wrestling place. "Open my eyes, Lord, to my hope in the gospel. Open my eyes to the riches in my account. Open my eyes to the power at work in me, the Holy Spirit, who is the same power that raised Christ from the dead. God, these things in my life are not like You! They do not reflect

Your kingdom come. How do I be godly and content with this? Am I supposed to encourage my friends to be content with this?!"

If by contentment I mean a passive acceptance, then no, I am not supposed to passively accept this, nor am I supposed to encourage my friends to passively accept such things. This is not the fullness of God's kingdom come! These things are not OK. But if by contentment I mean that I have faith that God has adequately supplied me and them through Christ's life, death, and resurrection; that He has sufficiently equipped us by lavishing on us a spiritual bank account with great equity to face these struggles head on; that the same power that rose Christ from the dead is now the power supernaturally at work in us, equipping us to deal with these struggles and empowering us as we wait for the fullness of Jesus's kingdom—if that is contentment, I understand why devotion to God coupled with that confidence is *great gain*.

That is my testimony. There was great gain to be had in those struggles, though it was not obvious at first. Such gain is counterintuitive, and it is not easily explained in tangible, physical terms. My friends that I mentioned would give similar testimony. There was a gain to be had as we waded through the pain of it all, and that gain was great.

Godliness with contentment is great gain in deep, hurtful circumstances. But it is also great gain in the daily grind of life. With lesser stressors, it is still life giving to remember these truths. I am devoted to God, and I want His kingdom to come in all its glory. Yet I am stressed with the little ways my life does not yet reflect His reign. In my own heart, the answer is to lean into Him, confident that He has sufficiently supplied me through His

Spirit to do good and not evil in big or small stressful situations. I am confident too that King Jesus is coming again to make all things right. The story is not yet finished.

Godliness with contentment does not mean pulling yourself up by your bootstraps. If the phrase fills you with guilt, you are missing the entire point. The gospel does not *obligate* you to contentment. It *equips* you for contentment. That battle with your sin, the temptation to gossip, anger with your children, church conflict, failing marriages, suffering, death—the gospel equips you to do battle with sin and suffering with the very same power that raised Christ from the dead. You have a lavish spiritual bank account, and this is an integral piece of the good news of all Christ has accomplished for you. Devotion to God coupled with such confidence in His sufficient supply is *great gain*.

Reflections

Chapter 4
The Gospel Gives Us Sanctuary

We were created in the image of God, jointly tasked with subduing the earth with our male counterparts, and specifically created as strong helpers who defend, protect, and care as God does for us. After the fall of man, Genesis 3 paints a stark outcome as the woman starts looking to the man she was created to help in the strongest sense of the word to meet needs in her heart only God could possibly satisfy. We discussed previously how the gospel equips us in a way a man never could. How exactly does the good news that Jesus is King do that? For one, Christ has made a way for us to have direct access to the God in Whom we are to find our satisfaction, to the One who sufficiently supplies us with our great spiritual inheritance at each turn in life. For an example of how the gospel does this and changes everything as a result, we will look deeper into the discontent Psalmist of Psalm 73 to which I referred in Chapter Two. Before I go through the psalm verse by verse, I encourage you to read straight through it for yourself.

Psalm 73 is clear about both the problem at the heart of mankind and the solution in the gospel. The Psalmist describes an age-old battle, the same battle that you and I face today. How can people who love God be content in this mess of a life?!

[1] Truly God is good to Israel,
  to those who are pure in heart.
[2] But as for me, my feet had almost stumbled,
  my steps had nearly slipped.

The Psalmist is at the end of his rope, barely hanging on. In theory, he knows the truth, that "God is good to Israel, to those who are pure in heart." His doctrine and theology are correct. But there is a disconnect between what he says he believes about God and his earthly reality. His theology of God, though true, seems inadequate for the issues he is facing. His emotional and spiritual exhaustion is palpable.

> [3] For I was envious of the arrogant
>   when I saw the prosperity of the wicked.
> [4] For they have no pangs until death;
>   their bodies are fat and sleek.
> [5] They are not in trouble as others are;
>   they are not stricken like the rest of mankind.

Why is the Psalmist at the end of his rope? It is the wicked and the arrogant. Evil doers are prospering. Though they die like everyone else, they do not seem to be suffering in life. Apparently, the Psalmist is watching righteous people, maybe personal friends, suffer while the wicked seem to get a free pass. That reality is undoing him.

> [6] Therefore pride is their necklace;
>   violence covers them as a garment.
> [7] Their eyes swell out through fatness;
>   their hearts overflow with follies.
> [8] They scoff and speak with malice;
>   loftily they threaten oppression.

The pride of evildoers is their necklace. They wear their pride and do not even attempt to fake humility. They are violent and get away with it. They mock and jeer others, perhaps directing it specifically to this psalmist. They "speak with malice," meaning that they threaten others out of sheer meanness. Their lives are characterized by foolishness.

> [9] They set their mouths against the heavens,
>   and their tongue struts through the earth.
> [10] Therefore his people turn back to them,
>   and find no fault in them.
> [11] And they say, "How can God know?
>   Is there knowledge in the Most High?"

Worst of all for the Psalmist who is trying to hang on to his fledgling faith, these wicked people "set their mouths against the heavens." They are not just shaking their rebellious fist at people on earth; they are shaking their fist at heaven. They mock God, and people seem to listen to them.

> [12] Behold, these are the wicked;
>   always at ease, they increase in riches.
> [13] All in vain have I kept my heart clean
>   and washed my hands in innocence.
> [14] For all the day long I have been stricken
>   and rebuked every morning.
> [15] If I had said, "I will speak thus,"
>   I would have betrayed the generation of your
>   children.

Note his summary of the wicked in verse 12. They are always at ease, increasing in riches. The Psalmist pours out his weariness in verse 13. In terms of godliness with contentment, which we discussed in Chapter Three, this Psalmist is definitely godly. His life is devoted to God. He is pious. He kept his heart clean, and he washed his hands in innocence. But it was vain, empty, and meaningless in his perspective.

According to verse 15, the Psalmist was feeling something

on the inside that he would not say on the outside because he knew if he verbalized it, it would seem a betrayal of everything he was supposed to believe. Does that sound familiar? It does to me. I have been there, at the end of my rope, barely hanging on, faking it on the outside because I do not want to betray God or those I love by acknowledging how vain, empty, and meaningless my belief in God seems at that moment.

Maybe you can identify with such despair. Perhaps you stood strong for a while during trying circumstances, but you got socked in the gut by life over and over while the wicked seemed at ease, increasing their wealth. Such seasons of life feel overwhelming.

> [16] But when I thought how to understand this,
>   it seemed to me a wearisome task,

The Psalmist is checking out. His devotion to God seems vain. It is more than he can process. He is too weary to try to understand it. Maybe he ignores it when he can and numbs himself when he cannot. What he cannot do is face it head on. It is too hard to reconcile, and he is too tired to deal with it. You likely know what he is describing—that moment when the disillusionment runs so deep in your heart you cannot even acknowledge it.

There are a number of moments in Scripture in which the Word paints a vivid contrast between our devastating need and God's overwhelming provision. Paul does this beautifully in Ephesians 2:1-5. This moment in Psalm 73 is another one. The state of the Psalmist's heart is stark. He seems hopeless. The desolation of verse 16 makes the provision in verse 17 incredibly beautiful.

^{17} until I went into the sanctuary of God;
  then I discerned their end.

He entered God's sanctuary! These are simple but profound words. As New Testament believers with the whole revelation of Jesus Christ, we can appreciate this even more today, for this is what Christ's death on the cross purchased for us. This is key to understanding the gospel and is worth a short diversion from Psalm 73 to explore how the New Testament sheds light on this dawn of new hope in the Psalmist's heart. The book of Hebrews in particular gives us great insight into this access to God we now have that changed everything in Psalm 73.

The Holy of Holies

In the Old Testament, the temple consisted of an outer courtyard in which the common people were allowed and an inner sanctuary in which only the priests were allowed. Within the inner sanctuary was the Holy of Holies. It housed the ark of the covenant, God's symbolic presence with His people. There was a thick veil between the Holy of Holies (or God's presence) and the area in which the priests were allowed. Once a year, the High Priest could enter the Holy of Holies with severe restrictions. He had to have a blood sacrifice. He needed to be purified. Even after these preparations, the other priests would attach a rope to his ankle so they could pull him out in the event he entered unworthily, and God struck him dead.

At Christ's death on the cross, He cried out at the climactic moment of His sacrifice, "It is finished!" Matthew 27:51 says, "At that moment the curtain of the temple was torn in two from top to bottom." The heavy, thick barrier between the children of

God and His symbolic presence with them was ripped apart. The doorway to God's presence was opened wide. Consider the implications of this moment according to the author of Hebrews.

> Hebrews 10 [19] Therefore, brothers, since we have confidence to enter the holy places by the blood of Jesus, [20] by the new and living way that he opened for us through the curtain, that is, through his flesh, [21] and since we have a great priest over the house of God, [22] let us draw near with a true heart in full assurance of faith, …

> Hebrews 4 [16] Let us then with confidence draw near to the throne of grace, that we may receive mercy and find grace to help in time of need.

In Christ, you and I can enter God's presence with confidence. We can enter boldly. We do not have to enter like Esther did with the king, fearing for her life. We do not have to enter bearing a new sacrifice or our good deeds. For a long time, I was tempted away from prayer at the very times I most needed to avail myself of this access to God. I would try to clean myself up or wait to pray until I had something to offer God. But that was, first, just theologically wrong and, second, self-defeating. It is the throne of grace, which implies that we need grace. It is the place where we find mercy, not the place we avoid when we most need mercy.

Just as Hebrews 4:16 indicates, our discontent Psalmist finds great mercy and grace in his time of need by entering the sanctuary of God. Look at all that changes, not in his circumstances, but in his perspective as this point of Psalm 73.

> [17] … then I discerned their end.
> [18] Truly you set them in slippery places;

you make them fall to ruin.
¹⁹ How they are destroyed in a moment,
   swept away utterly by terrors!
²⁰ Like a dream when one awakes,
   O Lord, when you rouse yourself, you despise
   them as phantoms.

I have a picture in my mind of the Psalmist wearing out-of-focus glasses that were distorting his vision of life. When he entered the presence of God, his lenses were readjusted and his vision restored. Now, he sees the prosperity of the wicked in an entirely different light. He discerns their end. He finally comprehends the truth of where the wicked are heading, and it is utter ruin. When God rouses Himself against them, it will be devastating.

Like the Psalmist, you will know when your perspective has been restored by the presence of God. It is that moment when you stop being jealous of the wicked and start feeling burdened for them. I have a close friend whose husband left her for another woman. It was horrible. The other woman had money that my friend did not, and for a long time it seemed just a bitter betrayal by her husband. I remember well the day her perspective changed, when she told me for the first time, not in anger or codependence but genuine compassion, how concerned she was for him and the path on which his choices were taking him. When you enter God's presence, you begin to recognize the terror of living apart from His presence. The grace and mercy God gives us at His throne of grace equips us to evaluate the wicked with compassion rather than envy, burdened for them rather than frustrated by them.

Paul teaches such compassion in 2 Timothy 2.

²⁴And the Lord's servant must not be quarrelsome but kind to everyone, able to teach, patiently enduring evil, ²⁵correcting his opponents with gentleness. God may perhaps grant them repentance leading to a knowledge of the truth, ²⁶ and they may come to their senses and escape from the snare of the devil, after being captured by him to do his will.

Paul reminds us that the wicked are not our ultimate enemy. They are enslaved by our real enemy. But only time in the presence of God will give us that perspective on our enemies and move us from vexation over their prosperity to concern for their final destination. We must avail ourselves of this great access we have to God and His sanctuary through Christ's sacrifice.

> ²¹ When my soul was embittered,
>   when I was pricked in heart,
> ²² I was brutish and ignorant;
>   I was like a beast toward you.

Not only is the Psalmist's perspective adjusted so that he sees the wicked clearly, he also has a clearer understanding of himself. In the Psalmist's head prior to entering God's sanctuary, he was just feeling sorry for himself. Now, he recognizes his bitterness and ignorance. He had been acting brutish—showing little intelligence or sensibility. He had been responding more like an animal than an image bearer of God. Have you had a moment when you came to your senses like that? I have.

> ²³ Nevertheless, I am continually with you;
>   you hold my right hand.
> ²⁴ You guide me with your counsel,
>   and afterward you will receive me to glory.

Nevertheless. I love that word. The Psalmist has been ignorant and bitter with God, yet he does not dwell in shame. He does not wallow in self-condemnation. Instead, he admits his sin and unbelief and walks forward in the truth hand in hand with God.

These verses remind me of the three pronged attributes of God that are foundational to His character. God is sovereign, God is wise, and God is compassionate.[17] Hear the love and compassion God has for the Psalmist. He holds him like a child by the hand. He guides the Psalmist with His wise counsel, and after this life, the Psalmist is confident that his sovereign God will take him to glory.

With his refocused perspective, the Psalmist has his eye on the eternal. Regularly throughout the Old and New Testaments, believers who overcame trials referred to their common belief that God was doing something bigger than their current circumstances. Consider Joseph's story from Genesis 37-50. We often focus on the earthly reconciliation to Joseph's struggles when his brothers show up in need of food to save their family from extinction. Yet, when the author of Hebrews references Joseph in the Hall of Fame of faith in Hebrews 11, it is Joseph's conviction that God was doing something that transcended Joseph's lifetime for which he is commended.

> [22] By faith Joseph, at the end of his life, made mention of the exodus of the Israelites and gave directions concerning his bones.

Joseph had such confidence that God's purposes for His children transcended their current struggles and that they were all a part of something eternal that he gave directions concerning

---

17   *Knowing God* by J. I. Packer explores these attributes of God in depth.

his bones!

Paul teaches a similar truth in Ephesians. Throughout the book, he refers to all that is going on "in the heavenly places." In Ephesian 1, we are blessed in Christ with every spiritual blessing in the heavenly places. Later in the same chapter, Christ is seated in the heavenly places. In Ephesians 2, Paul says that we too are seated with Him in the heavenly places. In Ephesians 3, the wisdom of God is being made known to rulers in the heavenly places. Then, in Ephesians 6, we are wrestling not against the wicked on earth, but with spiritual forces of evil in the heavenly places.

There is something going on outside our line of vision in heaven, and this eternal perspective is key to gospel-centered life on earth. That perspective is only accomplished through availing ourselves of our access to God's throne room, which is key to making sense of the rest of life. The prosperity of the wicked will crush you and me apart from such a view of God's eternal, transcendent purposes. We have to let our confidence in what is happening in that reality inform how we interpret what is happening in our earthly reality. That is key to the Psalmist's changed perspective in Psalm 73.

> [25] Whom have I in heaven but you?
> And there is nothing on earth that I desire besides you.
> [26] My flesh and my heart may fail,
> but God is the strength of my heart and my portion forever.

Here again, we see the answer to the problem of misplaced desires from the curse of Genesis 3:16. Women often look to men to meet deep seated needs in their lives that finite man was never intended to meet. But when we, male or female, enter the sanctuary of God and avail ourselves of the access to God that Christ's death provides for us, our desires get directed to the right Source of fulfillment. Our flesh may fail—we may be physically overwhelmed. Our heart may fail—we may be emotionally overwhelmed. But God is our strength and our portion forever. Portion means our legacy or inheritance, in those days a parcel of land that was endowed to provide for an heir. God is the Psalmist's inheritance. In Christ, God is our inheritance, our portion, as well. He has endowed us with Himself to provide for our deepest long-term needs and to equip us to help others in the strongest sense of the term.

In my own marriage, even to a faithful, loving husband, I must avail myself of the presence of God as my satisfaction and inheritance. My physical, emotional, and spiritual desires and needs are too much for Andy to bear. Andy is not my portion. He is not my inheritance. He is not the gospel. He is not the good news, and neither are my children. God is! Getting this is key at every place in the life of a woman who wants to live in the center of the gospel.

> [27] For behold, those who are far from you shall perish;
>   you put an end to everyone who is unfaithful to you.
> [28] But for me it is good to be near God;
>   I have made the Lord GOD my refuge,
>   that I may tell of all your works.

The Psalmist ends this chapter parked in the throne room. He has made the presence of God his refuge. This is where he hides. He gives an accurate summary of the condition of man apart from Christ in verse 27 and how God is his good supply.

The Psalmist is modeling for us godliness with contentment. He has an honest understanding of the problems of his world. His head is definitely not stuck in the sand. Though he has not yet heard of the Lord's Prayer, he longs for God's kingdom to come and His will to be done on earth as it is in heaven. He ends the chapter with the correct perspective on the tension between those things for which we righteously long and our earthly reality. Knowing that God has provided the Psalmist with God Himself as his rich supply has changed everything in his heart. Devotion to God coupled with confidence in His sufficient supply to meet the needs of the moment has been great gain in this Psalmist's life. May we too avail ourselves of our access to God Himself, who is our portion and inheritance that Christ's death on the cross has freely given us.

Reflections

Chapter 5
Equipped to Forgive and be Forgiven

The Psalmist of Psalm 73 demonstrates to us how availing ourselves of the presence of God radically changes our perspective on life. I want to zoom in for a moment on how this satisfaction we have in God as our great inheritance and His subsequent sufficient supply through the gospel equips us to deal specifically with others' sins against us and our sins against them.

Recently, someone in my life dropped the ball in a way that hurt me and hurt someone to whom I was ministering. Yet, despite the extenuating circumstances they could have used to excuse themselves, this person called me on the phone and told me how very sorry they were. They did not offer the other good works they were doing all week as an excuse for the problem that hurt me. They did not offer the family medical issues they were experiencing as justification. They simply said they were sorry and told me what they were going to do to repair things.

Why was concern, confession, and reparation the norm for this person? I know them, and simply, it was their theological understanding of the gospel. They were secure in Christ's finished work, and that confidence in Him freed them to say, "I made a mistake."

The gospel makes confession safe so it can be our normal response to sin and conflict. The gospel makes confession safe for me with my children, with my husband, and with my friends. It makes it safe when I am in authority, and it makes it safe when I am under authority. In Christ, owning up to my mistakes and seeking to repair what I have done wrong in my family or outside my home is no longer threatening to me. My standing with God does not rest on my performance, and I do not have to fake perfection in my family, particularly with my kids. I do not have to fear that my authority with them will be forever lost if I admit I was wrong. The truth is that I will most effectively undermine my gospel ministry to them if I instead circle my wagons in defensiveness and self-protection when I sin.

When I am faced with an accusation against me in my home or outside with others, I am often tempted to justify myself.

> Justify: to show by act or statement to be just or right, to defend or uphold as warranted or well-grounded. To absolve or acquit.[18]

Instead, I am already justified by God, though not by my own works. The friend whom I mentioned earlier who apologized to me was willing to admit their own mistakes without simultaneously needing to look to their good works to absolve themselves. Their response ministered much grace to me. Their apology was the apology of one who understands Romans 3 for themselves.

> [23]for all have sinned and fall short of the glory of God, [24]and are justified by his grace as a gift, through the redemption that is in Christ Jesus, [25]whom God put forward as a propitiation by his blood, to be received by faith. This was to show God's righteousness, because in his divine forbearance he had passed over former sins. [26]It was to show his righteousness at the present time, so that he might be just and the justifier of the one who has faith in Jesus.

18   Justify. Dictionary.com. Collins English Dictionary - Complete & Unabridged 10th Edition. HarperCollins Publishers. http://dictionary.reference.com/browse/justify (accessed: October 31, 2012).

God justifies us. He makes us right through Christ's righteous life and death. Then, He sufficiently equips us to face our sins head on without shame or condemnation. When I am justified by God, I do not need to justify myself to others. I do not need to absolve, acquit, or generally defend myself. I can say I am sorry for whatever I did that wounded another and begin the work of repairing and correcting it because the gospel equips me to let go of my reputation and empty myself of my rights.[19] When this kind of gospel belief slams up against serious pain and conflict, amazing, miraculous things happen, to the praise of God's glorious grace.

Most of us recognize that at some point we have made mistakes that have hurt others. Most of us have also been wounded by others' mistakes. I tend to prefer the term mistake when I am the one making it and the term sin when someone does it against me. However, the gospel equips me to handle both in straightforward ways that are honest about the pain I have caused and the pain I have received. Most importantly, I can be honest about the ways I have not obeyed God. The most beautiful, practical benefit I have personally experienced through the gospel is the freedom to lay down my personal need to defend myself with God or others. That freedom allows me to then offer the next person the freedom to lay down his or her defensiveness as well.

Defensiveness by definition is an excessive concern with guarding against the threat of criticism, injury to one's ego, or exposure of one's shortcomings.[20] In contrast, the Bible frees us

---

19 Philippians 2:5-8
20 Defensiveness. Collins English Dictionary - Complete & Unabridged 10th Edition. HarperCollins Publishers. http://dictionary.reference.com/browse/defensiveness (accessed: October 31, 2012).

to walk in the light and expose the truth of our wrongdoing so that we can then confess our sin to God and seek the forgiveness of others whom we have wronged.

> James 5 [16] Therefore, confess your sins to one another and pray for one another, that you may be healed. The prayer of a righteous person has great power as it is working.

> I John 1 [9] If we confess our sins, he is faithful and just to forgive us our sins and to cleanse us from all unrighteousness.

> Matthew 5 [23] So if you are offering your gift at the altar and there remember that your brother has something against you, [24] leave your gift there before the altar and go. First be reconciled to your brother, and then come and offer your gift.

Defensiveness and authentic confession of sin are mutually exclusive. They are incompatible. Yet, I have tried at times to include both in my attempts to reconcile with someone. I may say, "I'm sorry for [whatever], but you [had it coming]." Instead of stopping with a simple confession, I am tempted to add a justification of my actions at the end. To be frank, such self justification does not reflect what the Bible means by confession and repentance. We undermine the power of a sincere confession when we use language that both confesses sin and defends ourselves for why we did it. Instead, confession and repentance are solely about acknowledging our own personal sin. Confessional statements stop being authentic confession the moment we get distracted from our own personal sins and focus on what was done to us or said about us. Those things are relevant and should be addressed at some point. But we should not confuse them with authentic confession nor let them interfere with repentance.

What is repentance in the Bible? It is more than simple remorse or regret. It goes beyond mere sorrow. The Apostle Paul sheds light on this difference in 2 Corinthians 7.

> [9] yet now I am happy, not because you were made sorry, but because your sorrow led you to repentance. For you became sorrowful as God intended and so were not harmed in any way by us. [10] Godly sorrow brings repentance that leads to salvation and leaves no regret, but worldly sorrow brings death. NIV

Paul draws a distinction between good, godly sorrow that leads us to authentic confession and repentance and worldly sorrow that leads to death. Paul is not shy about the consequences of this sorrow that is not of God. It leads to destruction, and we are wise to understand what type of sorrow this is.

Worldly sorrow is characterized by feelings of shame, pain, or embarrassment that you got caught in sin. Along with that shame, you may feel hopelessness over ever being cleansed from your sin or able to repair the relationship with the person you sinned against. Such worldly sorrow may be relieved by someone else doing something for you or you doing something for yourself. Maybe you seek out someone to affirm you or distract you. You may try to manipulate how others think of you and look to them to make you feel better about yourself. If one relationship is broken, you may manipulate other relationships to replace the one you harmed.

In contrast, godly sorrow is sorrow that directs you to Christ. You do not need someone else to do something for you.

You do not need to do something for yourself. Instead, you fall flat on your face before God alone, for godly sorrow points you directly to Him. Godly sorrow is relieved by repentance and faith in what Christ has already done for you. Then, resting in what God has done for you, you can lay down your attempts to justify yourself to others. You can simply ask their forgiveness and repair with those you have hurt.

Many of us spend years of our lives mistaking worldly sorrow on a wide range of sin issues for authentic repentance and then wonder why we never change or why our relationships never heal. Feeling bad about what you have done is not the same as a godly sorrow that leads to repentance. God calls us to recognize our wrongdoing and need for forgiveness and then turn to God to forgive and correct it. We do not have to live in a perpetual state of regret and shame. Christ bore our shame and condemnation on the cross. His sacrifice for us equips us to face our sin head-on without fear that it will forever define us.

My first instinct is to feel more woe over others sins against me than I do over mine against them. But it is a good day when I shed defensiveness as the gospel equips me to do and face my sin with sincere apologies with no excuses attached.

> Psalm 32
> [5] I acknowledged my sin to you,
>   and I did not cover my iniquity;
> I said, "I will confess my transgressions to the LORD,"
>   and you forgave the iniquity of my sin."

Once I have faced my sin and confessed it without self justification, I am the person best equipped to extend forgiveness to others.

Ephesians 4 ³² Be kind and compassionate to one another, forgiving each other, just as in Christ God forgave you.

Colossians 3 ¹³ bearing with one another and, if one has a complaint against another, forgiving each other; as the Lord has forgiven you, so you also must forgive.

The Bible is clear that our forgiveness of others is inextricably tied to God's forgiveness of our own sins. These verses help us examine ourselves when we are faced with seemingly insurmountable anger and bitterness against another. Forgiving others when they have seriously wounded us is not easy. Many of us struggle with long term discouragement and even bitterness over old wounds by people we trusted. The best advice I ever received when I struggled with forgiving another person was, "Preach the gospel to yourself!" We struggle to forgive when we detach our forgiveness of others from God's forgiveness of us. It is only God's grace to us that can equip us to face the serious wounds others have brought upon us. I am inspired by Jesus' words in Luke 6 that give me a vision for this in my life.

> [31] And as you wish that others would do to you, do so to them. [32] If you love those who love you, what benefit is that to you? For even sinners love those who love them. [33] And if you do good to those who do good to you, what benefit is that to you? For even sinners do the same. [34] And if you lend to those from whom you expect to receive, what credit is that to you? Even sinners lend to sinners, to get back the same amount. [35] But love your enemies, and do good, and lend, expecting nothing in return, and your reward will be great, and you will be sons of the Most High, for he is kind to the ungrateful and the evil. [36] Be merciful, even as your Father is merciful.

When I studied through Ephesians for the last book I wrote, I noted the radical message that Jesus taught in Luke 6 about grace. The Greek word for grace, *charis*, is the word translated twice as benefit and once as credit in that passage. When you give back what is earned or deserved, it is not *charis*. It is not grace. Furthermore, it is not credited toward you as anything other than exactly what you are expected to do. Instead, grace does what is unexpected, undeserved, and out of line with reasonable responses. Grace is an unreasonably good response. When we give such undeserved favor that does good to enemies and lends expecting nothing in return, we give evidence of our relationship with our Father in heaven, because this is His calling card. He is kind to the ungrateful and evil. He is full of grace.

Grace is possibly the most often used but least understood word in Christian circles. I learned the acronym for grace, "God's riches at Christ's expense," in Sunday school as a child. But I did not understand grace. I understood that I did not earn my salvation, but my response was to start trying to earn it from that point forward. If God was that good to me, then I needed to start being a better person so that I could pay Him back a bit, or so I thought. But Jesus in Luke 6 sets a different criteria altogether as evidence of our understanding of grace. Jesus says the evidence of our understanding of God's grace toward us is our grace toward others.

When we get grace, we can then grant forgiveness. In Christian circles, we sometimes mistake other virtues for grace. I know many Christians who are diplomatic, generally friendly, or polite. But these traits are not the same as Biblical grace. Grace is an unreasonably lavish response to those undeserving of it, based on our own understanding of God's great, undeserved favor toward us. Examining God's grace to us is the prerequisite for us extending it to others. Grace is God's hallmark, and He is clear that a lack of forgiveness of others is inconsistent with His forgiveness of us.

If someone has expressed hurt or anger against you, I encourage you to truly believe that the gospel frees you from a need to circle the wagons and defend yourself. God circled the wagons 2000 years ago and accepted Christ's perfect sacrifice in the middle. Then He smashed the wagons. We do not need them anymore. God, through the gospel, protects us from being destroyed by another's accusations against us. He has freed us from our need for self-protection. We are equipped to face our sins head on as well as others' sins against us. Grace, mercy, and forgiveness are His trademark, and when we extend such grace, mercy, and forgiveness to the next guy, that is when we demonstrate to the world we are children of our Father in heaven.

> 2 Corinthians 5 [18]All this is from God, who through Christ reconciled us to himself and gave us the ministry of reconciliation; [19] that is, in Christ God was reconciling the world to himself, not counting their trespasses against them, and entrusting to us the message of reconciliation.

Reflections

Chapter 6
The Gospel Unites Us with Christ

The book of Ephesians is often called the "Queen of the Epistles." It is like a Reader's Digest condensed version of the whole story of redemption from Genesis to Revelation. In one short book, the Apostle Paul teaches in glorious detail what Christ's death on the cross accomplished for us, the seriousness of our need as sinners that caused God to do this, and the ways this gospel changes us practically. Paul presents in Ephesians a great manual on "gospel-centered" living. He uses the phrases *with Christ, in Christ, through Christ, with Him, in Him,* and *through Him* over thirty times in Ephesians' six short chapters. The gospel, we see, has not just given us access to God through Christ, but it has also included us in Christ. It has sealed us *in Him*—a phrase that would sound blasphemous if the Bible did not say it first.

> Ephesians 1 [13] In Him, you also, after listening to the message of truth, the gospel of your salvation—having also believed, you were sealed in Him with the Holy Spirit of promise. NAS

Our inclusion into Christ changes everything. It gives us a brand new identity—righteous, virtuous, and powerful—because it is His identity.

Our identity is our sense of self. It is the thing that gives us continuity in how we interact with others despite changes in our circumstances. We often identify ourselves by lesser things than how God identifies us. Some of us identify ourselves by our career, our relationship status, or our children. I have been a middle school, high school, and college math teacher, jobs in which I found a great deal of personal fulfillment. Now, I am a wife and mother. On the side, I am an author. Depending on the season of life, I have looked to each role to feel good about myself, to identify myself positively. But those are just roles I steward for a season. They are not my ultimate identity. Even being the daughter of a family firmly rooted for generations in the low country of South Carolina does not ultimately define me. Jesus Christ, along with all His name invokes, defines me both here on earth and for eternity in heaven. He is my identity because I am *in* Him.

Practically speaking, when I mix up my roles at any given stage of life with my ultimate identity, I end up in idolatry. At the stage of life I am now as wife, mom, and author, my husband and children cannot be my identity. I cannot pin all of my hopes for the future on their personal successes. It is not fair to them, and it keeps me from placing my hope for the future in God's hands. They become my idols when I do that. I also cannot place my hopes for feeling good about myself on the books I write. It did not take long after publishing my first book to receive criticism from a reviewer. I figured out quickly that I would be undone if I allowed the way my books were received to make me feel good or bad about myself. Instead, God calls me to be a good steward of my roles of wife, mom, and author, not an idolater who looks to her husband, children, or books (or whatever stewardship God has given at the time) for her sense of personal achievement.

The problem with idols is not that they *will not* affirm us and satisfy us in the way that we long. The problem is they *cannot*. It is not in their power. We devastate relationships in our lives when we look to certain people to meet needs in us God never intended them to meet. A spouse, friend, or child may try for a season to fill those needs and make us happy, but at some point, they will become so discouraged by the utter depth of our need and our inability to be satisfied with anything they do that they will push us away, perhaps even severing the relationship completely.

Jesus alone is our ultimate source of identity. But what exactly does it mean for us to find our identity in Christ? The Bible uses several word pictures which I find helpful to communicate the details of our relationship with Christ. The Word paints believers at multiple places in Scripture as, first, Christ's cherished bride.[21]

> Hosea 2 [16] "And in that day, declares the LORD, you will call me 'My Husband,' and no longer will you call me 'My Baal.' ...[19] And I will betroth you to me forever. I will betroth you to me in righteousness and in justice, in steadfast love and in mercy.

The Bible also gives the illustration of Christ as the vine in which believers are the branches ...

> John 15 [1]"I am the true vine, and my Father is the vinedresser. [2] Every branch in me that does not bear fruit he takes away, and every branch that does bear fruit he prunes, that it may bear more fruit .... [4]Abide in me, and I in you. As the branch cannot bear fruit by itself, unless it abides in the vine, neither can you, unless you abide in me. [5] I am the vine; you are the branches. Whoever abides in me and I in him, he it is that bears much fruit, for apart from me you can do nothing."

---

21   See also Revelations 21.

... and Christ as the Head and believers as His body.

> Ephesians 1 ²² And God placed all things under his feet and appointed him to be head over everything for the church, ²³ which is his body, the fullness of him who fills everything in every way.

All three of these illustrations point to the intimate union between Christ and His church. Colossians 1:17 says that Christ "is before all things, and in Him all things hold together." We are in Him, and He holds it all in unity. If you belong to God, then you are supernaturally connected to Christ along with all of God's children.

Instead of seeing myself as connected to Christ at all times, I used to view my relationship with God in terms of intersecting moments during the day. The more times my life intersected with God in a given week, the more "spiritual" I thought I was. In that paradigm, God went on His way and I went on my way until we intersected at some corner on some future day. Instead, I have learned to think of myself walking with Jesus continually, twenty-four hours a day, seven days a week. Our daily walk together is not just parallel but actually intertwined. I, of course, do not take full advantage of that walk with Him all day every day, but I am learning that it is indeed my reality, and the more I am aware of it, the more stable I am emotionally and spiritually. If you are a believer, God is with you, in you, holding you together at all times. The goal is for us to be aware of that reality and live like it is true, for Christ warns us that apart from Him we can do nothing.

In John 15 when talking of the vine and branches, Christ says, "Abide in Me." The Greek word for abide is *meno*, meaning to remain, tarry, be held, or be kept continually. There are two mental pictures in the Bible that seem to contradict each other. We just discussed those pictures that show us united with God the Son, Jesus Christ. But the Bible also invites us to boldly and confidently enter the presence of God the Father at His Throne of Grace.[22] Instead of contradicting each other, these pictures enhance each other in my mind. We are children of God who are both passively connected to God and actively encouraged to seek His presence. These dueling images of abiding free us from both legalism and apathy. I am kept secure in Christ through no work of my own, yet God calls me to actively participate in using the resources provided to me through this union.

Christ is my perfect Bridegroom. I am connected to Him as a branch is to a vine and as a body is to its head. From Him, I get the nourishment I need to live out my part in His larger story. He is the answer to the misplaced desires predicted for women in the curse of Genesis 3:16. He nourishes, sustains, and equips you and me. God, through Jesus, affirms us, speaking deep words of grace and purpose over us. The core longings of our hearts for relationship and identity are perfectly fulfilled in Him. I encourage you to take time at the end of this chapter to read the entirety of Paul's beautiful description in Ephesians 1 of the blessings from this union we have with Christ.

> Ephesians 1 ³ Blessed be the God and Father of our Lord Jesus Christ, who has blessed us in Christ with every spiritual blessing in the heavenly places, ⁴ even as he chose us in him before the foundation of the world, that we should be holy and blameless before him. In love ⁵ he predestined us for adoption as sons through Jesus Christ, according to the purpose of his will, ⁶ to the praise of his glorious grace, with

---

22 Hebrews 4:16

which he has blessed us in the Beloved. [7] In him we have redemption through his blood, the forgiveness of our trespasses, according to the riches of his grace, [8] which he lavished upon us, in all wisdom and insight [9] making known to us the mystery of his will, according to his purpose, which he set forth in Christ [10] as a plan for the fullness of time, to unite all things in him, things in heaven and things on earth.

[11] In him we have obtained an inheritance, having been predestined according to the purpose of him who works all things according to the counsel of his will, [12] so that we who were the first to hope in Christ might be to the praise of his glory. [13] In him you also, when you heard the word of truth, the gospel of your salvation, and believed in him, were sealed with the promised Holy Spirit, [14] who is the guarantee of our inheritance until we acquire possession of it, to the praise of his glory.

Reflections

Section 3
Wisdom in the Tension

Teachers who present Scripture's instructions to women apart from the gospel set women up for failure. That is a strong statement, but consider Paul's words in 2 Corinthians 3.

> [5] Not that we are sufficient in ourselves to claim anything as coming from us, but our sufficiency is from God, [6] who has made us sufficient to be ministers of a new covenant, not of the letter but of the Spirit. For the letter kills, but the Spirit gives life.

Apart from the gospel, the law kills. I have sat under much teaching that crushed women through law, seemingly oblivious to Christ's provision and the Holy Spirit's empowerment. I have done this to others at times in my own teaching as well.

Often in my experience, teachers did not just present the law on women's issues, but they also presented their own personal application of it. The law says tithe, but the legalist pressures others to tithe their spice rack. As a new wife, I felt constrained by others' applications for their families of general Bible principles. My husband finally had to tell me point blank, "Honey, I don't need that!" I was stressed over color coordinated, organic meals when he just needed clean socks. I was greeting him in a state of anxious self-condemnation over the clutter in our home when he is actually more comfortable in clutter than in a precisely organized room. But no one clarified for me the difference in general Bible principles and personal application, or the Spirit's role in guiding in either.

We need wisdom in the tension as we navigate daily life knowing what God created us to be in perfection as strong helpers versus the reality of our earthly struggles—longing for what God declared good, yet living abundantly in Christ until His kingdom comes, and He restores all that lacks in our lives. In this section, I distinguish between wisdom and law, especially on women's issues. Then I look at Christ's fulfillment of the law and the Bible's own guidance on how we can receive both Old and New Testament instructions.

In that context, we will look at various passages that offer wisdom from God and examples from Christ on navigating this life. Some of these passages, such as the verses on the Proverbs 31 wife, have ministered more condemnation than grace to me over the years because I did not understand the passage with the clarity that Christ and the gospel now offer me. But when the good news of Christ's life, death, and resurrection is the filter through which we read these instructions, they can minister great grace to us as we navigate this broken world.

Chapter 7
Wisdom Versus Law

In Chapter Three, we walked through the phrase godliness with contentment and explored the sufficiency the gospel gives us for facing all the ways our personal lives and larger world do not yet reflect God's good purposes for His children. We will never exhaust our need to meditate on this concept and apply it in our lives. In a recent sermon, my pastor defined the gospel as everything that the life, death, and resurrection of Christ accomplished for us, and this gospel changes everything. Subsequently, the entirety of the Christian walk is figuring out, for a lifetime, all the things the gospel changes about ourselves and the ways it changes them. This is as true for women as any other demographic in the church.

As we navigate Scripture's instructions to women, we must first distinguish between wisdom and law and second between universal law and law for a specific culture for a specific time. Once we understand the difference in wisdom, Old Testament law, and universal Biblical instruction, we can understand how the gospel equips us to repent when we miss the mark and walk forward in renewed obedience.

One of my favorite passages in all of Scripture is Luke 24. It is a key passage for unraveling how the gospel informs our understanding of all other instructions in Scripture. While it says a lot, it alludes to even more. I would love to know what else was said during the parts of the conversation not recorded in this chapter.

The setting is the dusty road to Emmaus, several miles from Jerusalem. Jesus has died. Someone is spreading a rumor that He has come back to life, but Luke says most received it as an "idle tale" and did not believe it. Two of Jesus' followers are walking along the road discussing all that had happened—Jesus' short but flamboyant ministry, His miracles, their former confidence that He was the one predicted by the prophets to free Israel from oppression, and His crucifixion, which shook everything they thought they understood about Him. They thought Jesus was going to rescue them from Roman oppression and be their King. Wasn't that what the Messiah was supposed to do? Whatever they thought He was going to do, being put to death on the cross by Roman soldiers seemed to unravel everything.

As they talk, Jesus draws near to them and begins walking with them, but they do not recognize Him. He asks them what they are talking about. They look sad according to Luke and start explaining that Jesus was . . .

> [19] a man who was a prophet mighty in deed and word before God and all the people, [20] and ... our chief priests and rulers delivered him up to be condemned to death, and crucified him. [21] But we had hoped that he was the one to redeem Israel. Yes, and besides all this, it is now the third day since these things happened. [22] Moreover, some women of our company amazed us. They were at the tomb early in the morning, [23] and when they did not find his body, they came back saying that they had even seen a vision of angels, who said that he was alive. [24] Some of those who were with us went to the tomb and found it just as the women had said, but him they did not see.

Jesus responds to them,

²⁵"O foolish ones, and slow of heart to believe all that the prophets have spoken! ²⁶ Was it not necessary that the Christ should suffer these things and enter into his glory?" ²⁷ And beginning with Moses and all the Prophets, he interpreted to them in all the Scriptures the things concerning himself.

Later Jesus instructs them,

⁴⁴ "These are my words that I spoke to you while I was still with you, that everything written about me in the Law of Moses and the Prophets and the Psalms must be fulfilled." ⁴⁵ Then he opened their minds to understand the Scriptures, ⁴⁶ and said to them, "Thus it is written, that the Christ should suffer and on the third day rise from the dead, ⁴⁷ and that repentance and forgiveness of sins should be proclaimed in his name to all nations, beginning from Jerusalem."

Note that the climax of whatever specific things Jesus told them about Himself through the Law, the Prophets, and the Psalms is that Christ should suffer and rise again and that "repentance and forgiveness of sins should be proclaimed in His name" in all places. This is the culmination of the message of the Old Testament.

We are about to wade into some of the hardest passages for women in Scripture, starting with Proverbs 31. We must understand what Jesus means in Luke 24 and use this good news to navigate how we apply Scripture and avail ourselves of its instructions.

Proverbs is the wisdom literature. Solomon was the wisest man to live. Yet even Solomon, who wrote much wisdom on raising children and finding a virtuous wife, did not excel at either. The author of the wisdom literature couldn't keep his own advice. But Christ did.

> 1 Corinthians 1 [30]And because of him you are in Christ
> Jesus, who became to us wisdom from God, righteousness
> and sanctification and redemption.

Christ is the personification of the wisdom of God. He is the righteousness of God. He redeems us, and He sanctifies us. This is the incredible news of the gospel—in Christ there is no condemnation.[23] Just as we bear no condemnation as we wear His robe of righteousness, we bear no condemnation because we are in Him, and He is our wisdom.[24]

As we read through the wisdom literature of Proverbs 31, think of Jesus becoming for you this wisdom of God. Make no mistake—Proverbs 31 contains great wisdom! It is great advice from on high. It is wonderful counsel. And it is fulfilled in the Wonderful Counselor. Do not be indicted by the ways your life does not fit Proverbs 31. Maybe it is an impossible passage for you because of your life circumstances. Your children cannot rise up and call you blessed if God has not given you children, right? The heart of your husband cannot safely trust in you if God has not brought a husband into your life. Or maybe you have a husband and children, but the gulf between the virtuous wife of Proverbs 31 and your reality threatens to swallow you up in hopelessness. Please do not go to that dark place.

In Christ, this wisdom of Proverbs is not just possible, it is already your status in heaven. This is wisdom from God, and it is not here to taunt you. Inspire you? Yes! Give you insight as the Holy Spirit brings these passages to mind in specific situations in

---

23 Romans 8:1
24 Isaiah 61:10, 2 Corinthians 5:21

your life? Yes. But not to frustrate you or condemn you. Guilt and condemnation are lousy motivators. Instead, Christ has become for us the fulfillment of this wisdom from God, and He then empowers us to live wisely.

Furthermore, wisdom is not law. Christians often confuse wisdom and law, Proverbs and the Ten Commandments. But there is an obvious difference. There are no opposite laws or opposite commandments! Yet we are all familiar with opposite proverbs. Look before you leap, but he who hesitates is lost. For a Biblical example, consider Proverbs 26:4-5.

> [4] Answer not a fool according to his folly,
>   lest you be like him yourself.
> [5] Answer a fool according to his folly,
>   lest he be wise in his own eyes.

Wisdom is not law, and wisdom is only wise when applied correctly in the right situations. We cannot read Proverbs the same as the Ten Commandments, yet in the fight against ignoring Scripture, we sometimes fear situational wisdom. The result is often silly, one-dimensional applications.

The answer to our fears of moral relativism is to apply wisdom in ways that are actually wise through the indwelling Holy Spirit. Paul exhorts us in Galatians 5:16 to "walk by the Spirit," which literally means to "keep in step with the Spirit." It is this pressing into God via the Spirit that equips us to apply wisdom in wise ways without fear of moral relativism. It equips us to distinguish principle from application and to know what application God has for us as opposed to what He has for some other person in a different situation.

However, many believers are suspicious of the Holy Spirit.

At times, I think I would rather have spent three years with Jesus in person as Peter did than twenty years indwelt by the Spirit. Yet, if we compare Peter after his years in Jesus' presence with Peter after time with the Holy Spirit, we see clearly, as Jesus Himself says, that it was better for Peter, resulting in greater growth and maturity in his life, that the Spirit indwell him than he continue to sit in person at Jesus' feet. It is a profound truth.

> John 16 [7] Nevertheless, I tell you the truth: it is to your advantage that I go away, for if I do not go away, the Helper will not come to you. But if I go, I will send him to you. [8] And when he comes, he will convict the world concerning sin and righteousness and judgment … . [13] When the Spirit of truth comes, he will guide you into all the truth,

In the context of, first, the difference in wisdom and law, second, God's wisdom fulfilled in us through Christ, and third, the profound influence and power of the Holy Spirit in us, we will look at Proverbs 31. But before we do, we need to understand a little bit more about law in Scripture.

Reflections

Chapter 8
The Bible is the Best Commentary on Itself

Before we go any further in our discussion of gospel-centered womanhood, we need to establish what the Bible does and does not say to women today. Receiving the Word of God as God intended is a fundamental act of faith. In my early days at college, I first faced my belief (or unbelief) in the trustworthiness of the Scripture handed down by the Church for thousands of years. Could I trust the Bible I held in my hands? How did I know it was true? What about the questions others regularly raised? I studied how we got our texts for a while in college, but at some point I realized that I could not study my way out of the need to take a step of faith on the reliability of Scripture.

I took that step of faith and believed that the Bible was what it claimed—the living, trustworthy revelation of God to His people, a revelation that transcends any particular cultural context. Yet, I still wondered what to do with peculiar passages that seemed totally irrelevant for me today. I knew early on in my wrestling over Scripture that I did not want to rely on myself to determine what was and was not relevant for me today. It seemed foolish for me to choose to accept the parts of the Bible that I liked and reject the parts I did not. Thankfully, the Bible did not leave me as an orphan to navigate that on my own. In fact, the Bible gives great insight to us on how to interact with it. The Bible is the best commentary on itself, and we are wise to examine the various things it reveals to us about itself.

At times, God wrote out His revelation of Himself in the form of stories. Sometimes, He used clear commands and instructions. Within those clear commands and instructions, God gave universal truths for all cultures and all times along with instructions that played a specific role for a finite period of time. The question then is how does Scripture reveal what parts were for a particular time and what parts transcend time or culture?

Most believers agree that not all parts of Scripture should be literally followed today, as evidenced by the fact that no modern Christian group offers animal sacrifices. However, beyond animal sacrifices, there are divergent perspectives within the larger evangelical movement on how we know what is required for today, especially in terms of application to women. It is tempting for me to rely on my own cultural understanding as the basis for what does and does not apply to me in Scripture. But the Bible transcends cultural context. The Bible makes audacious claims about itself. It claims to be living.[25] It claims to be trustworthy for the long haul.[26] It speaks to events that occurred well before it was first written and to those that will occur long after it was completed. Most of all, it claims that each human writer was ultimately carried by the Holy Spirit to say what God Himself, not the human writer, inspired them to say.

> 2 Peter 1 [20] Knowing this first of all, that no prophecy of Scripture comes from someone's own interpretation. [21] For no prophecy was ever produced by the will of man, but men spoke from God as they were carried along by the Holy Spirit.

---

25 Hebrews 4:12
26 Matthew 5:18

The most important insight the Bible gives us for understanding itself is that Jesus' life and death fulfilled the Old Testament Law. We already read Jesus' teaching in Luke 24 that all of the Law and Prophets pointed to Him. In Matthew 5:17, Jesus also teaches something specifically about the Old Testament Law, which says some things to women that we may be tempted to write off simply due to their weirdness. He says, "Do not think that I have come to abolish the Law or the Prophets; I have not come to abolish them but to fulfill them." He states this previous to His death and reinforces an impossible standard, that we need to keep the Law better than the Pharisees. After His death, Paul teaches that Jesus alone was the only one who could keep the Law as God intended, and His death marked the great exchange that we discussed earlier. We are now counted as having kept the Law as Jesus did! Christ is the end of the Law for all who believe in Him.[27]

The Law served several purposes. It served to show civilization what God values. We value the dignity of human life, care of the poor, fidelity in marriage, fairness in business dealings, social justice, and so forth because God first showed us through the Law that He cared about such things. Also, the Law showed from multiple different angles both our need for a Savior and what He would look like when He comes.

Some Christian groups distinguish between categories of the Law such as ceremonial, sacrificial, and moral law. But the Bible does not make such distinctions, and I find those distinctions confusing rather than helpful. There are many wrong ways to think about Old Testament laws. They should not be written off,

---

27 Romans 10:4

ignored, or abolished. Instead, Jesus *fulfilled* them. He brought them to completion, and their purpose is concluded. Much of the books of Galatians and Hebrews are spent exploring this point.

> Galatians 3 [23] Now before faith came, we were held captive under the law, imprisoned until the coming faith would be revealed. [24] So then, the law was our guardian until Christ came, in order that we might be justified by faith. [25] But now that faith has come, we are no longer under a guardian,

In the book of Hebrews, the author quotes Jeremiah who says the Law is now written on our hearts.[28] What God did externally through His Law in the Old Covenant, He now does internally through the Holy Spirit in the New Covenant.

Not only did Jesus fulfill the Law, He boiled it down for us so that we could continue living in the essence of what the Law was meant to convey to us about God's character and His desires for His children. Jesus summed this up with the Golden Rule and Greatest Command.

> Matthew 7 [12]"So whatever you wish that others would do to you, do also to them, for this is the Law and the Prophets."

> Matthew 22 [36] "Teacher, which is the great commandment in the Law?" [37] And he said to him, "You shall love the Lord your God with all your heart and with all your soul and with all your mind. [38] This is the great and first commandment. [39] And a second is like it: You shall love your neighbor as yourself. [40] On these two commandments depend all the Law and the Prophets."

After studying portions of the Old Testament Law over the

---

28 Hebrews 10:16

years, I have a new appreciation for God's purposes and protections to His children by way of them. There was no government but God at the time. His instructions through the law encompassed much more than simple morality as we perceive it today. There was no Food and Drug Administration or Occupational Safety and Health Administration. God gave this law at the dawn of civilization, and at that point, civilization was not very civilized. What kind of instructions were needed for people dealing with the most basic of dietary and sanitary needs? For instance, it makes sense that God would instruct His people in Leviticus 11 not to eat bottom dwelling shellfish, the scavengers of the ocean. Even today, despite modern refrigeration and testing for bacteria, people often get sick from eating them. How much greater the risk for God's children who had no refrigeration and no ability to test for bacteria.

That instruction is a fairly easy one to understand. There are others that are not. Some instructions simply seem odd. Others seem downright brutal. We do not know God's exact reason for each, but understanding that God was giving basic instructions at the dawn of civilization to people with no government, police, or medical help gives insight into their general purpose.

Not only is the Old Testament Law fulfilled in Jesus, there is another helpful principle for understanding Scripture. Bible story is not the same as Bible instruction. Some Scripture passages describe what happened while others prescribe what we are to do. Just because the Bible tells a story does not mean we are to emulate the details of that story.

The book of Judges is helpful in demonstrating the difference. There, God describes ugly things in Israel's history,

95

and He does it without much discussion of whether the things described are good or evil. At the end of this story, He writes, "In those days there was no king in Israel. Everyone did what was right in his own eyes."[29] The description in Judges serves to show the need of God's children for the true King of Kings who would save them from their depravity.

Combining these principles for reading Scripture, we start to get a clearer picture of how to receive the Word on any subject, especially the topic of gospel-centered womanhood. We start in Genesis 1 and 2 where God states in perfection that every woman is an image bearer of God reflecting especially His strong help and advocacy for His children. From there, I recommend studying Ephesians, where Paul lays out our spiritual inheritance via the gospel as the key to once again being the "imitators of God" that He created us to be.[30] In between, the Old Testament Law pointed toward Christ and was fulfilled in Him. Proverbs 31 gives insight, wisdom, and understanding (not law), which is best received under the press of the Holy Spirit who helps us apply it in ways that are actually wise in our own lives as opposed to the conclusions some may espouse when they try to convict us in place of the Spirit. The New Testament reaffirms the summary moral code of the Ten Commandments. Jesus even intensifies it in His Sermon on the Mount. The essence is summed up in the Greatest Command and Golden Rule. Much of the epistles then flesh out what such love looks like in the New Covenant, and we can trust those instructions even as we wrestle with the Holy Spirit to understand and apply them.

---

29 Judges 21:25
30 Ephesians 5:1

Reflections

_____
_____
_____
_____
_____
_____
_____
_____
_____
_____
_____
_____
_____
_____
_____
_____
_____
_____
_____
_____
_____
_____
_____
_____
_____

Chapter 9
Wisdom from Proverbs 31

As we begin our look at Proverbs 31, remember the context we set up in the last two chapters. There is a difference in wisdom and law, Christ is the personification of God's wisdom fulfilled in us through the good news of the cross, and we now have the indwelling Holy Spirit walking with us in this process of applying wisdom.

The virtuous wife of Proverbs 31 reflects back on the first woman created in the image of God in Genesis 2:18 to be a helper to her husband. God is called the helper of His people throughout Scripture, and the first woman was gifted at creation to reflect particular aspects of His strong advocacy and care for His children.[31] But the helper created in Genesis 2 was marred deeply by the fall of man. The battle of the sexes began. Supportive relationships, especially between spouses, became the exception rather than the norm, evidenced throughout the rest of Genesis in the stories of Sarah, Rachel, Leah, and so forth.

While the Proverbs 31 wife reflects back to the first woman created in perfection, she also reflects forward to the wife of Ephesians 5 who, redeemed by Christ, is equipped to reclaim the image of God in her relationship with her husband. In Paul's beautiful discourse on the gospel in Ephesians, he tells in the first two chapters God's plan before time began to redeem back all

---

31   Exodus 18:4, Psalm 10:14

that was lost in the fall of man. Then, in the opening of Ephesians 5, we see that, in Christ, we are now equipped to be "imitators of God," once again living as the image bearers of God that He created us to be.

In that context, Paul paints a picture at the end of Ephesians 5 of what marriage looks like between husbands and wives who are *in Christ* and *image bearers of God*. Both are tasked with gospel love for the other. Though the husband is called to give a special example and manifestation of this love, make no mistake that both the husband and the wife are commanded to love. Both are also tasked with mutual service and deference. Just as the husband is called to give a specific example of love, the wife is called to give a specific example of submission. But, again, each is called to defer to one another. The context of these instructions is crucial. Removing this teaching from the gospel context Paul clearly presents undermines them completely. Paul's instructions to husbands and wives are fully founded on what it looks like to imitate God in marriage by way of Christ's sacrifice for us.

Proverbs 31 gives us a similar picture of the kind of love and support that a woman who is in Christ and an image bearer of God can provide in her home. She is a precious gift to her husband, valued far above earthly riches.

Some translations refer to this female as the virtuous or capable *woman* rather than the virtuous or capable *wife*. The Hebrew word can mean either, but wife seems the better translation in context. Otherwise, this chapter makes it sound that the pathway to virtue for a woman is singularly through a husband and children. But Scripture is the best commentary on itself, and it gives us the story of Ruth among others to clarify this false notion. Ruth's virtue and capable nature are most clearly evident as a single widow with no children. Well before Boaz came into the picture, Ruth is everything in character that God has called her to be. Rather than serving as a taunting, unattainable goal to single women who love and serve Christ, the virtuous wife of Proverbs 31 is a model for those who are in marriages tainted by the fall who long for a practical vision of what is possible in their marriages and homes through Christ.

Before we discuss the principles this passage addresses, I encourage you to read the entire passage.

Proverbs 31
[10] An excellent wife who can find?
   She is far more precious than jewels.
[11] The heart of her husband trusts in her,
   and he will have no lack of gain.
[12] She does him good, and not harm,
   all the days of her life.
[13] She seeks wool and flax,
   and works with willing hands.
[14] She is like the ships of the merchant;
   she brings her food from afar.
[15] She rises while it is yet night
   and provides food for her household
   and portions for her maidens.
[16] She considers a field and buys it;
   with the fruit of her hands she plants a vineyard.
[17] She dresses herself with strength
   and makes her arms strong.
[18] She perceives that her merchandise is profitable.
   Her lamp does not go out at night.
[19] She puts her hands to the distaff,
   and her hands hold the spindle.

^{20} She opens her hand to the poor
   and reaches out her hands to the needy.
^{21} She is not afraid of snow for her household,
   for all her household are clothed in scarlet.
^{22} She makes bed coverings for herself;
   her clothing is fine linen and purple.
^{23} Her husband is known in the gates
   when he sits among the elders of the land.
^{24} She makes linen garments and sells them;
   she delivers sashes to the merchant.
^{25} Strength and dignity are her clothing,
   and she laughs at the time to come.
^{26} She opens her mouth with wisdom,
   and the teaching of kindness is on her tongue.
^{27} She looks well to the ways of her household
   and does not eat the bread of idleness.
^{28} Her children rise up and call her blessed;
   her husband also, and he praises her:
^{29} Many women have done excellently,
   but you surpass them all."
^{30} Charm is deceitful, and beauty is vain,
   but a woman who fears the LORD is to be praised.
^{31} Give her of the fruit of her hands,
   and let her works praise her in the gates.

From this description, we see that the virtuous wife is *for* her husband. She does him good, not evil, all his days. She is also *for* her family. She is aware of their needs and is diligent to support, protect, and encourage them. The great summary statement of the entire section on the virtuous wife is found in verse 30, "a woman who fears the LORD is to be praised." Her horizontal relationship with her husband and family is based on her vertical relationship with God. She remains in close relationship with her

God, for without Him, she can do nothing.[32] That is what gives her the peace to face her future with laughter and joy.

The Proverbs 31 wife can inspire us no matter our marital status. The author of this proverb (most likely Solomon, but possibly not) paints a picture of a woman who is right with God and right with others. She seems at peace internally though she has many burdens to bear and battles to fight. Those values certainly transcend marital status though the specific applications are focused on her husband and family.

Instead of going through the meaning of each individual verse, I would rather focus on the big nuggets of wisdom in this chapter through which the more specific descriptions flow. Consider verses 11 and 12, which are foundational to the rest of the description of this wife.

> [11] The heart of her husband trusts in her, and he will have no lack of gain. [12] She does him good, and not harm, all the days of her life. ESV

> [11] The heart of her husband trusts in her confidently and relies on and believes in her securely, so that he has no lack of [honest] gain or need of [dishonest] spoil. AMP

These verses remind me of the concept of a stumbling block, which is a way the Bible refers to spiritual hindrances or obstacles. The wisdom here is that the virtuous wife is not a stumbling block to her husband. She does not set up her husband for failure.

If you believe in the sovereignty of God, stumbling blocks may be a confusing concept. I personally have a strong belief in

---

32   John 15:5

the sovereignty of God and His irresistible grace. I trust my sovereign Father in heaven to woo my heart to Him. I trust Him to woo my children. I trust Him also to draw my spouse to God. Woe to me if the heart of my husband or my children depends on me. Their heart and spiritual condition are God's territory, and He takes responsibility for them. Yet, He calls me to join with Him as a steward. I can hurt my children and husband, and I can help them. Our God, who is sovereign over the heart of our families, also calls us to positive, active participation in this venture. We must hold to the two—both stewarding responsibility in our homes without living in condemnation for our failures like we are the ultimate reason they rise or fall. Only a firm grasp of the gospel can enable us to hold to the two.

In Proverbs 31:11, the author uses two simple yet deep words to communicate the character of this virtuous wife. The *heart* of her husband *trusts* in her. The Hebrew word for *heart* indicates the core of the man's inner workings—his mind, will, and understanding. It represents the seat of his emotions. The Hebrew word for *trust* is an inspiring word. It means to have confidence, boldness, and security. Something about the character of this wife causes her husband to trust her with his emotional center. He feels safe and can even be careless with her. He can let down his guard because he trusts her.

I am encouraged by this vision of a woman who can be trusted with her husband's heart, the place that holds his innermost fears and desires. She is a safe place for her husband to let down his defenses and be honest about his concerns. Yet, of all the wisdom in Scripture, this is probably the thing that came least easily in marriage for me, while it is also the thing that has made the greatest difference once I started to understand it and believe in its value.

Early in my marriage, I could not handle my husband's burdens because of my own fears. I did not want to ultimately be in control of our marriage, though women are often accused of such a thing. However, my fears of failure and lack of trust in God played out with attempts at manipulation and control at certain points in my marriage. In my experience, manipulation and control tactics are ineffective methods for dealing with our fears. They cannot begin to touch the root of our fears.

Instead of being a safe place for my husband to share his burdens, I can feel threatened by his burdens, concerns, and struggles. I want him to provide a security for me he was never intended to provide. When that happens, I have to reevaluate my faith and trust in God. I find that meditating on God's sovereignty is key to bringing me back to faith and trust in God so I can be a safe place to hear my husband's burdens each time these fears arise in my heart.

Isaiah 46
[9] "remember the former things of old;
  for I am God, and there is no other;
    I am God, and there is none like me,
[10]declaring the end from the beginning
    and from ancient times things not yet done,
  saying, 'My counsel shall stand,
    and I will accomplish all my purpose,'
[11]calling a bird of prey from the east,
    the man of my counsel from a far country.
  I have spoken, and I will bring it to pass;
    I have purposed, and I will do it."

Colossians 1 [17] He is before all things, and in him all things hold together.

Now, when I meditate on God's sovereign control over my family's circumstances and the profound truth that He holds all things together, I can turn toward my husband as the strong helper God intended me to be when He created me in His image, hear my husband's burdens without being threatened by them, and in so doing, minister great grace back to him as Paul's inspiring exhortation in Ephesians encourages us.

Ephesians 4 [29] Let no corrupt communication proceed out of your mouth, but that which is good to the use of edifying, that it may minister grace unto the hearers. KJV

If I were to summarize the benefit of Proverb's description of the virtuous wife, I would say she is a picture of wisdom in action in her home. The wise wife is *for* her husband and *for* her children. But beyond that broad summary, how should we interact with the specifics qualities mentioned in this chapter?

- She works willingly with her hands.
- She brings her food from afar.
- She rises while it is night to provide food for her household and maidens.
- She plants a vineyard.
- Her lamp does not go out at night.
- She makes linen garments and sells them.
- She looks well to the ways of her household and does not eat the bread of idleness.

The first observation that comes to my mind is that the

specific actions for which the virtuous wife is praised are not universally applicable. Few who teach from Proverbs 31 would pressure women to make shirts of linen or plant their own vineyard. My second observation is that she manages her house with help. For some reason, my perception of her from my early years of marriage and motherhood was that she did all this by herself, and I therefore should too. But the picture of wisdom here is of a wife managing her home rather than simply doing all of the specifics herself. According to verse 15, she has multiple young women or maidens helping her. One of the best decisions I made for my home the last few years was getting help with cleaning once we were in a position financially to do it. Initially, I felt guilt that I needed help. I felt I was abdicating my responsibilities. Instead, the help I received actually encouraged me with my responsibilities in my home.

However, those types of observation about the specifics of the virtuous wife do not do justice to the genre of Proverbs. It is wisdom, not law, and wisdom is only wise when it is applied correctly in the right situation. Wisdom is dependent upon the Spirit's leading and application. None of us should draw conviction about either hiring help in our homes or doing it all ourselves from simply reading my observations on this chapter. This is wisdom read in light of the finished work of Christ on the cross. The question should be how the gospel of the One who has become God's wisdom in and for us then empowers us to receive the specific descriptions in Proverbs 31 and apply its wisdom in our own lives.

I have most struggled with the description in verse 27 that "she looks well to the ways of her household and does not eat the bread of idleness." Those words have taunted me for decades, inducing guilt in my heart from early in my teenage years. Whatever eating the bread of idleness means, I have always felt that I am a glutton. I was the notoriously messy one growing up at home and later in my dorm room during college. I like to think I am mentally organized, but I have never come close to being physically organized. I felt condemned when I read how the capable wife tended well to her home. But in Christ, there is no condemnation for me on this issue.[33] Verse 27 is not a law. It does not instruct me to repent if I spent longer than fifteen minutes on Facebook or thirty minutes reading a magazine. Instead, it is wisdom that reminds me of my responsibilities and inspires me to complete them.

When I wrestle with the virtuous wife's example on idleness, I have to remember other parts of Scripture that teach on rest and celebration. As I said before, the Bible is the best commentary on itself. God spoke as law, not wisdom, that we need to set aside a day each week to rest and worship. Most Christians have noted the worship portion of that law, but fewer have understood the rest portion. The wisdom offered through Proverbs 31 is not that rest or downtime is a problem. On the contrary, rest and downtime are such valuable commodities in a believer's life that God set aside an entire day of the week for it.

Also, though Proverbs 31 warns against idleness, this is not the same as a warning against simply sitting with and enjoying others. God set up many festivals and celebrations for the purpose that His children remember and enjoy Him and His provision for them. For a day, a week, or even a year, His

33   Romans 8:1

children would accomplish nothing of long term physical value, yet such times were never characterized by God as idleness without eternal value. The story of Mary and Martha in Luke 10 reinforces this truth.

As I put together these pieces of the Word of God through the Spirit's inner working in my heart, I get a vision for my home that inspires me as opposed to one that merely guilts me. I said before that guilt is a lousy motivator, and I find it is rarely helpful for actually implementing wise ways to spend my time. Instead, the Spirit whispers through my heart suggestions of proactive engagement in my home that also allow for rest and worship, celebration and remembering.

Whatever piece of the wisdom of Proverbs 31 that particularly resonates with you, either positively or negatively, engage the Spirit with Bible study and prayer over it. Make certain that it is He that is convicting you and not another woman that He has led to apply it in a way that is only wise in her home, not yours. While guilt is a lousy motivator, the Spirit whispering through the Word is not. He will lead you well to apply this wisdom in ways that are wise for the home and relationships to which He has called you.

Reflections

Chapter 10
Instructions from Ephesians

Proverbs 31 paints a picture of a woman who is a safe place for her husband. Both Proverbs 31 and Ephesians 5 give us visions of what is possible in a marriage between two believers redeemed by God. Let's look more closely at Paul's description in Ephesians 5 of a marriage that is *in Christ* between *imitators of God*.

Paul first gives an overarching context that is not limited to either husbands or wives but should characterize all those who are in Christ. All should "walk in love," with Christ who "gave himself up for us" as our model (v. 2). All should have a high view of sex and walk in the light (v. 3-9). All should be characterized by a thankfulness to God and a reverence for Christ that equips us to defer to one another in general and submit to our own authorities in particular (v. 20-21).

Only then does Paul finally mention the particulars of husbands and wives, using the controversial word *submit* particularly with wives and the happy word *love*, which rarely invokes controversy, with husbands. Of course, all are called to love. Wives are as responsible to fulfill the Greatest Command with their husbands as husbands are with their wives. Husbands too are tasked along with each believer in the Body of Christ with humble self sacrifice. Every husband is called to serve his wife, as she is called to serve him. Yet, there is a specific manifestation of submission that Paul directs to wives along with a specific manifestation of love that Paul directs to husbands.

The Greek word for submit has a slightly different connotation than other words the New Testament uses for sacrifice and service. It is used of Jesus with his parents and those under the command of officers in the military. It means to arrange in order under the direction of a leader. I like the English word submission because its etymology gives insight into the term. *Sub* is from the Latin word for under. *Mission* indicates an important assignment. Someone has a mission, and someone else is supporting them from beneath. If you will allow me a cheesy music reference, the wife in this vision of marriage is the wind beneath her husband's wings, supporting his important assignments.

When I submit to my husband, I get on board with his mission. This is rarely of note in our home, because he and I are on mission together. But occasionally, our missions contradict or counteract each others. When there is conflict in our missions, God's instruction is that I bring my mission under that of my husband.

For an example from my marriage, since writing my first book, my public ministry has grown. I am often invited to speak to people I do not know in locations away from home. My husband values relationships closest to home as our family's first mission. My conviction is that Paul's instructions in Ephesians 5 are relevant for me today, and I often contemplate how to honor this passage in my home. A primary practical result in my life is that I bring my public ministry under our family's private ministry. I start with my husband and children, because I believe they are my first ministry. But I too have bought into my husband's vision for knowing and loving people in our immediate neighborhood, relationships I would have missed if I had not willingly positioned my public ministry under this burden we share for private relationships.

My application of this passage may be helpful to you at one level. However, at another level, my application is completely irrelevant to you. The Spirit, not me, is the One to lead you in what it looks like to imitate God in your own marriage. He will lead you in the ways that support your husband in his mission and burdens with strong help, care, and advocacy.

Paul's instructions to wives in the last verse of Ephesians 5 enlighten and reinforce both the vision given in Proverbs 31 of a wife who is a safe place for her husband and the one in Ephesians 5 of a wife who submits out of reverence for Christ. Paul gives us a single word, *respect*, that conveys deep wisdom on how practically to be this safe place. This too is a controversial word, especially since it is aimed at women without a corresponding instruction to husbands. Do only men need respect? Don't women need it too? Peter actually does instruct husbands to honor their wives in I Peter 3:7, though the word he uses has a slightly different emphasis than the word Paul uses for respect in Ephesians 5.

Similarly to the word submit, the most important thing to note about the word respect in Ephesians 5 is that it is in a context.

Ephesians 5 [1]Be imitators of God, therefore, as dearly loved children [2] and live a life of love, just as Christ loved us and gave himself up for us as a fragrant offering and sacrifice to God ....

⁸ For you were once darkness, but now you are light in the Lord. Live as children of light ⁹ (for the fruit of the light consists in all goodness, righteousness and truth)¹⁰ and find out what pleases the Lord ....
²¹ Submit to one another out of reverence for Christ.
²² Wives, submit to your husbands as to the Lord. ²³ For the husband is the head of the wife as Christ is the head of the church, his body, of which he is the Savior ....
²⁵ Husbands, love your wives, just as Christ loved the church and gave himself up for her ....³¹"For this reason a man will leave his father and mother and be united to his wife, and the two will become one flesh." ³²This is a profound mystery—but I am talking about Christ and the church. ³³However, each one of you also must love his wife as he loves himself, and the wife must respect her husband.

Paul has just used the same Greek word for respect, *phobeo*, in verse 21. "Submit to one another out of *reverence* for Christ." The Greek word means to fear, reverence, or treat with deference. That definition does not help it sound less controversial. If you are a woman with any sense of pride, your body likely tenses with dread in the pit of your stomach as you read those words. Such a definition at first seems at odds with any kind of self worth or self value.

Can only women with a low self image show such respect to their husbands? Can only women without their own valuable opinions submit to their husbands? We only have to look at it from the opposite perspective to clear that up in our heads. What attitude would you as a woman want from someone showing you respect? With maturity in life, we realize the ugliness of deference from someone with a low view of themselves. But when someone whose opinion I value shows respect to me, it is

114

meaningful at a profound level. When the strong helper made in the image of God offers respect to her husband, the meaning of that respect is compounded tenfold by the strong character of the giver.

I have at times been tempted away from offering respect to my husband because I perceived myself as making better decisions than him on certain issues. Such a mindset raises an important question. Which comes first, respect or respectability? I remember well an illustration given by an education professor during my undergraduate studies. He told of a junior high math teacher who, on the first day of class, mistook her students' locker numbers for their IQs. For the entire school year, she treated the students as if they were only as smart as their locker numbers indicated. Sure enough, at the end of the year, they had consistently lived up or down to her expectations.

This illustration reflects well the issue at hand with respecting our husbands. If I wait until my husband meets some subjective, external standard I have set for earning my respect, I will never respect him. I would be quite offended if my husband chose not to love me as Paul teaches husbands in Ephesians 5 until I met an external criteria he had set for being lovable. I would be very offended if he said I had to *earn* his love. Yet, I have at times approached respect exactly that way. As I have grown older, I have come to receive instructions to respect my husband as great wisdom from the Master Psychologist, God Himself, who knows better than anyone how His created sons best function mentally. Respect is my husband's love language. Our husbands need and long for our respect the way we need and long for their love. It ministers to them. It meets them in wounded places in their heart.

How do we respect someone if we have deemed them unworthy of our respect? This points back to that earlier question—which comes first, respect or respectability? Can we trust God's instructions to us on this issue? Even if our spouse seems to abdicate his responsibilities or does not live up to our expectations, when we honor him as God intended him to be, not as he is now (or as we perceive him to be), we are being salt and light in our marriage, powerfully influencing our husbands, not by nagging and manipulating, but by trusting God's wisdom. A godly wife's respect for her husband despite his fallen nature and tendency toward sin is a powerful tool of God to minister grace to her husband.

Sure, you or I may at times have a more logical, systematic argument for which car we should purchase or job we should take. And certainly there is a time and place to make that argument. But understand too when your argument stops being for your idea and against, maybe even mocking, his. Most importantly, recognize that your husband's conformity to God's image is more important than that car or whatever decision you are making. God's purposes in our marriages extend well past the earthly circumstances that will consume us if we let them. The car is irrelevant compared to our husband's heart and conformity to Christ, and a wife's respect is apparently in God's sight a valuable piece of the puzzle in terms of conforming a husband back to the image of God.

I have found Peter's instructions in I Peter 3 helpful on the subject of respect. At first, Peter's words sound even more controversial than Paul's in Ephesians 5.

1 Peter 3 [1]Likewise, wives, be subject to your own husbands, so that even if some do not obey the word, they may be won without a word by the conduct of their wives, [2]when they see your respectful and pure conduct.

I observe several important things about these verses from I Peter 3. First, there is something winning about submission and respect. The Greek word for won, *kerdaino*, can also mean gain or profit. The context involves a husband who is disobeying the Word. This is a very serious issue. Peter is teaching that in this serious situation, respect is a powerful response that wins over your opponent. Note that he does not say it defeats him. The difference in defeating and winning over is profound.

Some women may not want to win over their husband. Given enough hurt or anger, they may rather defeat and destroy, leaving a scorched earth in place of their conflict. In that case, this Scripture will only chafe against that desire. But if you love your husband and do not want to see him destroyed even as he walks a disobedient path, then respect is God's powerful weapon for winning him. There is gain and profit to be found in this respect, which is more powerful than words according to this passage.

Note also that this chaste, respectful response in the face of disobedience is not the same as sweeping a husband's sin under the carpet. This passage does not encourage a wife to ignore sin or pretend like it does not exist. That response does no one any good. The entire point of the passage is that this husband is clearly disobeying, and Peter's instruction is not that the wife pretend he is not. There are two unhelpful reactions to a husband's sin, and the first one is ignoring or minimizing it. Our culture calls it enabling. The second unhelpful reaction is one that relies on words over quiet character and strength. A wife may need to draw a line in the sand in light of her husband's ungodly behavior, but Peter's instruction indicates that fewer words are better.

The other thing to note about I Peter 3 is the very first word, likewise, which indicates that the thought Peter is presenting builds upon another thought. Like Paul in Ephesians 5, Peter has written these instructions to wives in light of something else, and the worst thing we can do is read these two verses without looking back at the context in which Peter is writing them. In the previous chapter, Peter made his case for sacrificial service and submission throughout the Body of Christ, arguing for it with these words.

> I Peter 2 [21] For to this you have been called, because Christ also suffered for you, leaving you an example, so that you might follow in his steps. [22] He committed no sin, neither was deceit found in his mouth. [23] When he was reviled, he did not revile in return; when he suffered, he did not threaten, but continued entrusting himself to him who judges justly. [24] He himself bore our sins in his body on the tree, that we might die to sin and live to righteousness. By his wounds you have been healed. [25] For you were straying like sheep, but have now returned to the Shepherd and Overseer of your souls.

Peter's next words are, "Likewise, wives...." When read in context of all of I Peter (as well as Ephesians 5, Luke 24, and Genesis 2), we see that the wife's calling is simply to be like Christ. Christ is both our model and our source of strength to obey on this matter. He is the wisdom of God for us, and we are in Him.

No discussion on submission and respect in the Christian home is complete without addressing cases of abuse. How do we apply these passages with a husband who cares nothing about imitating God? Remember again that Scripture is the best commentary on itself, and elsewhere God is clear on our responsibility to obey governmental authorities.[34] If your husband is unsafe, it is good and right to report him to appropriate authorities and remove yourself from the situation. If children are involved, your responsibility to do so is compounded.

Submission that is forced is not submission at all. Even in Paul's context, in which women had few rights or safeguards, he addresses wives as free moral agents with a choice in the matter. Forced subjugation is oppression, not submission, and in God's common grace to all people, He has allowed great movement in legal protections of women and children from abuse and oppression, particularly in western civilization. If your husband is participating in illegal, abusive behavior toward you or your children, remove yourself from the situation.

By understanding how the gospel supplies us in the places in our lives that do not yet reflect His goodness and His kingdom, we can be the strong helper God intended even in the muck of it all. A strong helper in the image of God is not an enabler. She does not give opportunity for abuse, and she does not turn a blind eye toward it. A Christian wife can love her husband unconditionally yet still remove herself from his illegal behavior. If you find yourself in an abusive situation, may your confidence

---

34 Romans 13

in your identity in Christ and God's great grace at work on your behalf give you boldness to act as you need to hold your spouse accountable.

> 2 Corinthians 9 [8]And God is able to make all grace abound to you, so that having all sufficiency in all things at all times, you may abound in every good work.

Reflections

Chapter 11
The Gospel in Your Context

Many Christian books aimed at women focus application on a woman's family and home, assuming that the average reader of such books has a husband and children or will one day. To a degree, I have done this as well. At least, I have written much application for wives and some for mothers. I have not, however, *assumed* that the average reader is a wife or mom. My own personal experience of singleness and infertility keeps me from making that assumption. Since getting married and having kids of my own, my many friends who are single, divorced, or widowed, with and without kids, remind me that the assumption that if you are not currently married or the parent of children that you will be one day is not particularly helpful at this moment in their journey.

The gospel surely is as meaningful for single women as it is for married ones, right? But in terms of outright instructions in the Bible aimed specifically to women, most passages in Scripture use the context of marriage and family. Depending on which statistics you read, even in modern society after the sexual revolution of the last few decades, around 75% of women will have married by the time they are thirty-five. There is a reason that much Biblical instruction to women centers on the issue of family.

However, there is another interesting way Scripture addresses women—not through instruction, but through story.

While much of the outright instructions to women in the Bible involve the context of traditional marriage and family, the actual stories of women in Scripture are quite varied. God gives us a broad sampling of women's stories with various backgrounds and influences affecting their circumstances.

Sarah and Rebekah are each the wife of one husband, while Rachel and Leah share a husband in a polygamous relationship. There is Abigail, the wife of a very bad man, who shows her character by going behind his back to avoid war with King David, and Esther, the young, single virgin who goes on to save her nation after marrying an unbelieving, oppressive king. Ruth is a barren widow caring for her mother-in-law, and Naomi is the mother-in-law who had lost both husband and children. Mary and Martha were single sisters of Lazarus who loved and served Jesus, while Priscilla had a husband she helped in ministry.

With no mention of husbands or fathers, Lois and Eunice raised their grandson and son, Timothy, in the faith. Phoebe helped Paul in ministry, possibly by relaying the book of Romans to the church at Rome. With no mention of her situation, we do not know if she was married or single, with kids or without, though she seemed to have freedom to help Paul in a way someone with a young family would not. There is also Mary the mother of Jesus, Mary Magdalene, the woman at the well, Rahab, Lydia, and Deborah. Scripture uses women with a wide variety of backgrounds and circumstances as integral pieces in the telling of God's redemptive story.

When a believing woman in 21ˢᵗ century America writes on Biblical womanhood, it is hard to break free of her own context. As an author, I may offer application for women who are not at the same stage of life as myself, which I can do in part because I know and love many friends not at my stage of life who freely share their burdens, concerns, and wisdom with me. But to break past that and offer application for women outside of my westernized culture with its many civil protections is something I have not yet been able to do well.

The Bible in contrast does address women of broadly different backgrounds at various stages of life. The redemption offered by Christ transcends cultural context and stage of life in ways in which a mere human author like myself can only begin to comprehend. I want to end this book by exploring in my own limited way how the gospel equips women at all stages of life from any background to live as image bearers of God in their particular context.

For the rest of this chapter, I make a big assumption — that the majority of women reading this without healthy family relationships still long for them. I use the phrase "without healthy family relationships" because there is a wide variety of relational experience outside of the traditional view of Christian family and home. In my own group of Bible loving friends, I know widows and divorcees, some in despair over their second or third divorce. Some friends have never gotten married and never had kids. Several have never married but do have children. Single parents often have an especially hard time finding their bearings in the western Christian church. Many women I know have strained relationships with their adult children. Into the twilight of their life, the struggle for healthy family relationships remains a burden. Despite the variety of their current circumstances, I rarely meet a Christian woman, young or old, who does not ultimately long to be married to a man who loves God and His Word and raise children who love Him too.

Our longing may be for a loving spouse or for healthy children. Perhaps we long for reconciliation with a former spouse or our adult children. Or maybe we are at peace with our marital status but long for harmony in other relationships. The question for each of us is what do we do with the lack in our lives? What do we do when we want something that God Himself says is good, something for which He seems to have instilled a longing within us, that He also seems to withhold from us?

This reminds me again of the discussion in Chapter Three of godliness with contentment. There I emphasized how the gospel equips us to face the lack in our lives—those things in our lives that seem to war with our hopes for life under King Jesus. Our God lives in His own perfect community, Father, Son, and Holy Spirit, and then He created us to live in His extended community as cherished sons and daughters. The sadness we feel over broken relationships with our parents, siblings, friends, children, ex-husbands, or current husbands, or the loneliness we feel because neither husband nor children ever entered our life in the first place are not wrong emotions. Much remains broken in the world at large and our individual lives in particular. Estrangement and loneliness hurt, and it is right that we long for more.

In my Bible, Romans 8 has the subtitle *Life in the Spirit*. There, Paul describes many beautiful facets of life in the Spirit. There is no condemnation for us who are in Christ Jesus (v. 1). We are set free from the laws of sin and death (v. 2). The mind

126

set on the Spirit is life and peace (v. 6). We are children of God (v. 14) who have been adopted by God (v. 15). In fact, we are co-heirs with Jesus Christ (v. 17), a position that would sound blasphemous if God did not say it Himself in Scripture. Right in the middle of this discussion of the blessings of having God the Spirit living in us as the guarantee that God is not going to default on His promises to us, Paul says this.

> [18] For I consider that the sufferings of this present time are not worth comparing with the glory that is to be revealed to us. [19] For the creation waits with eager longing for the revealing of the sons of God. [20] For the creation was subjected to futility, not willingly, but because of him who subjected it, in hope [21] that the creation itself will be set free from its bondage to corruption and obtain the freedom of the glory of the children of God. [22] For we know that the whole creation has been groaning together in the pains of childbirth until now. [23] And not only the creation, but we ourselves, who have the firstfruits of the Spirit, groan inwardly as we wait eagerly for adoption as sons, the redemption of our bodies. [24] For in this hope we were saved. Now hope that is seen is not hope. For who hopes for what he sees? [25] But if we hope for what we do not see, we wait for it with patience.

We are waiting with eager longing for something promised, groaning with creation as we wait to experience in our bodies and our lives the fullness of all Christ has accomplished for us. We have the *firstfruits* of the Spirit. In other words, we have begun to experience the first results from our union with Christ, but there is much greater profit ahead for us. Therein lies our hope. By definition, hope is for something that is not yet realized.

We do not yet experience in our reality all that God has prepared for us. In the meantime, we hunker down, waiting with patience for the fullness of this promised future grace.

Scripture uses two key words when giving instructions for living in this middle place where we have tasted the firstfruits of what God has accomplished for us through Christ yet still wait for the final fulfillment of all He has promised. Those two words are *wait* and *endure*.

Wait

God often uses waiting in Scripture to accomplish His purposes. He gives us many examples in His Word of believers on whom He called to wait—Abraham, Sarah, Jacob, Joseph, and Hannah to name a few. Their time of waiting on God's hand was an integral part of their walk with God, and the results of their waiting on God were fundamentally important not just to their individual lives but to God's eternal plan for the redemption of all His children. It is human nature to think of periods of waiting as holding patterns with no discernible value. Instead, Scripture teaches that there are blessings to be had in the actual waiting period.

> Isaiah 40 [31] but they who wait for the LORD shall renew their strength; they shall mount up with wings like eagles; they shall run and not be weary; they shall walk and not faint.

> Lamentations 3 [25] The LORD is good to those who wait for him, to the soul who seeks him.

Isaiah 30 [18] Therefore the LORD waits to be gracious to you, and therefore he exalts himself to show mercy to you. For the LORD is a God of justice; blessed are all those who wait for him.

According to these verses, waiting for the Lord to move in our lives is a good thing. There are blessings for those who wait for Him and renewal to be found in the waiting. Scriptures likens this renewal to a bird lifting off the ground and soaring through the air. But what do we do in the waiting? How do we deal with the fears that buzz around our heads or the despair that threatens to derail our daily lives?

Married or single, with kids or without, waiting for unfulfilled desire is a lifelong problem. Sometimes we desire things in opposition to God. Dealing with those types of sinful desires is hard, but it pales in comparison to the struggle of dealing with God-given desires that remain unfulfilled. Why would God impress on our hearts the value and worth of healthy, gospel-centered relationships without also fulfilling that desire? What do we do in the waiting with such unfulfilled desire? The Word of our sovereign Father in heaven is to be still and fret not.

Psalm 37
[7] Be still before the LORD
   and wait patiently for him;
 fret not yourself over the one who prospers in his way,
   over the man who carries out evil devices!

Be still. It is OK to sit down and rest. I remember the constant fear I had as a single woman that I was going to miss my chance at God's best for my life. I did not have the strong conviction I now have that my sovereign God had a plan for my life that He, not me, had promised to accomplish. Subsequently, a few months after breaking up with a good man whom I could not talk myself into marrying, I despaired that I had lost my one chance at happiness. It did not help that well-meaning Christians could not understand why I did not marry him. I realize now that there are many godly men out there, and just because a particular man is a good guy does not mean he is the right guy for me (or you). It was God's good plan for that guy as much as myself that I did not marry him.

Short of a strong confidence in a sovereign Father who has a good plan for our lives for which He bears the responsibility, we can feel pressure to strategize and manipulate to change our circumstances. In my life, such strategies did not accomplish much of help except to keep me occupied. I have found great value at multiple turns in my life in simply resting. Seasons of waiting, when I take my hands off the steering wheel and remove my foot from the gas, have been some of the sweetest of my life. I shut my laptop, turn off the phone, and sit still for a while without pressure on myself to change my situation. My journal bears witness of those seasons, where I cry out to God, and He speaks words of peace to me. Wait. Rest. Be still. In the waiting, He will lead us beside still waters and restore our soul as only the Good Shepherd can do.

Psalm 37:7 also instructs, "Fret not." The Hebrew word for fret is translated other places *become angry* or *distressed*. Picture a person worrying, with mannerisms that fluctuate between anger and distress. I have been there, concerned over some circumstance that I am alternately angrily trying to manipulate or despairing over my lack of control. In contrast, God calls us to confidence and peace. How do we move from anxiety to peace in concerning circumstances? I know of no other way than to review what I know to be true about God and then to take my thoughts captive and make them submit to the truth.

> 2 Corinthians 10 [5] We destroy arguments and every lofty opinion raised against the knowledge of God, and take every thought captive to obey Christ,

What do I know of the character of God? In a nutshell, God is sovereign, wise, and compassionate.

> Psalm 135 [6] The LORD does whatever pleases him, in the heavens and on the earth, in the seas and all their depths.

> Romans 11 [33] Oh, the depth of the riches and wisdom and knowledge of God! How unsearchable are his judgments and how inscrutable his ways!

> Psalm 103 [13] As a father shows compassion to his children, so the LORD shows compassion to those who fear him.

God is in charge, and He knows what He is doing in your life. You can trust that He has not lost control of your circumstances. Not only does God know what He is doing, His plan for your life reflects both His all-surpassing wisdom and His fathomless love for you. His plan is good and right, and you can trust Him with the details of your life.

After reviewing what you know to be true of the character of God, I encourage you to avoid the pitfall of comparing yourself with your sisters in Christ who are dating, engaged, or happily married with kids. They did not get married or have kids because they have it all together, and God does not ask you to wait because you are unworthy. The Bible says that such comparisons between ourselves and others are not wise. They do not help in any way.

> 2 Corinthians 10 [12] We do not dare to classify or compare ourselves with some who commend themselves. When they measure themselves by themselves and compare themselves with themselves, they are not wise.

If you must compare yourself to someone, compare yourself to Christ. We were created in God's image and are now being conformed back to it through Christ. There is no other standard of righteousness for our Christian lives. I thank God for women who are examples of godliness to me, but I do not use them as my standard of righteousness. Instead, Christ is my standard of righteousness, of which I certainly fall short, yet which God also determined before time began to conform me to His likeness.

> Romans 8 [29] For those God foreknew he also predestined to be conformed to the likeness of his Son, that he might be the firstborn among many brothers.

In our waiting, we can rest and fret not because our sovereign and wise Father in heaven has great compassion for us. He is in control, He loves us, and He knows what He is doing. These are key facts that empower us to...

Endure

Romans 5 [2] Through him we have also obtained access by
faith into this grace in which we stand, and we rejoice in
hope of the glory of God. [3] Not only that, but we rejoice in
our sufferings, knowing that suffering produces endurance,
[4] and endurance produces character, and character produces
hope, [5] and hope does not put us to shame, because God's
love has been poured into our hearts through the Holy Spirit
who has been given to us.

Hebrews 12 [1] Therefore, since we are surrounded by so
great a cloud of witnesses, let us also lay aside every weight,
and sin which clings so closely, and let us run with
endurance the race that is set before us,

When studying through the book of Hebrews recently, I was
struck by the way the author ends the book. He gives a long
exhortation to believers on the topic of endurance. Hebrews 11 is
often called the Hall of Fame of faith because it gives a list of
men and women from the Bible who lived as aliens and strangers
on earth, looking at God's promises from afar while enduring in
hope until the end of their lives. This cast of characters remains
today as a cloud of witnesses around you and me, cheering us on
from the sidelines. The author of Hebrews then exhorts us to
look to Jesus, the author and finisher of our faith, as we, like
those who have gone before us, run with endurance the race that
is set before us.

There is something about this particular cloud of witnesses
that encourages me. They lived their own version of this struggle
with unfulfilled godly longing well before I came into the picture.
They testify to me that, indeed, this world is not my home, but

they do so in a way that does not cause me to despair. Our eternal hope is real, and this cloud of witnesses stands in joy experiencing the full benefits of all it means to be a child of God. They exhort me from the sidelines to continue in hope of my very real inheritance whose firstfruits I have just begun to taste on this side of heaven. Even when that first taste has faded, it has nevertheless whet my appetite for the very good fulfillment that is eternally secured for me in heaven. This hope—this expectation of something real that is waiting for me—is the thing empowered by the Holy Spirit that sustains me to endure my alienation on earth for the long haul, having experienced only the firstfruits of all God has promised.

As I conclude this short study on the ways the gospel equips us to live as overcoming women in fallen circumstances, I encourage you, dear sister in Christ, to endure. Put one step in front of the other without giving up. Stand strong, alternately planting your feet while bracing against the storms of life and moving one foot forward in those moments the wind dies down, always believing confidently that your sovereign Father will keep His promises to you. He has not left you as an orphan to endure this season of waiting for the resolution between your godly desires and your earthly reality. He has left His precious Spirit in you as the deposit that guarantees He will not default on His promises to you.

> Ephesians 1 [13] In him you also, when you heard the word of truth, the gospel of your salvation, and believed in him, were sealed with the promised Holy Spirit, [14]who is the guarantee of our inheritance until we acquire possession of it, to the praise of his glory.

There is much good news for us as daughters of God made in His image to strongly help those in our care. We have tasted the firstfruits of this good news and are sufficiently equipped to run with endurance until we experience the bloom of the whole. We will acquire possession of it, and the Spirit is God's guarantee over our lives. To the praise of His glorious grace.

> Run, John, run, the law commands
> But gives us neither feet nor hands,
> Far better news the gospel brings:
> It bids us fly and gives us wings.[35]

---

35 Attributed to John Bunyan.

Reflections

Discussion Questions

If you are participating in a group study of *The Gospel-Centered Woman*, here are suggested questions for discussion.

Introduction

1. "Something had invaded the boundaries of their lives, decimating their naïve notions of how their lives would play out" (page 1). Have you had a similar experience in your own life?

2. How does Matthew 11:28-30 apply to you in light of situations you are currently facing?

Chapter One

1. What do you think God meant when He said He would make a helper suitable for Adam?

2. Who needs this kind of help, why do they need it, and when do they need it?

Chapter Two

1. Have unhealthy desires toward a man been a part of your life? How?

2. Has a need for affirmation affected your relationship with men? With women? In what ways?

3. Have you attempted to manipulate or control others in your life similar to the women of Genesis? Have others tried to manipulate or control you? What was the outcome?

Chapter Three

1. What parts of your life and relationships seem at war with your desire for God's will to be done?

2. What are your reflections on 2 Corinthians 9:8 for yourself in your current circumstances?

3. Has this chapter changed your perception of the phrase "gospel-centered?" Describe what that phrase means to you.

Chapter Four

1. In what ways do you identify with the Psalmist's struggle in Psalm 73?

2. How did entering the sanctuary of God change the Psalmist's perspective?

3. What does entering the sanctuary of God look like for you as a believer in the 21st century?

Chapter Five

1. Have you circled the wagons in a defensive response to another? Did it help reconcile the situation?

2. How does the gospel enable you to lay down defensiveness?

3. Is there someone you need to forgive? Someone from whom you need to ask forgiveness?

Chapter Six

1. We have been "sealed in [Christ] with the Holy Spirit of promise" according to Ephesians 1:13. What does this mean to you, and how does it impact how you think of yourself and your struggles?

2. Of the three pictures of Christ and believers (husband and wife, vine and branches, and head and body), which impacted you most and why?

3. What does it look like in practical terms for you to abide in Christ?

Chapter Seven

1. Explain the difference in wisdom and law in the Bible.

2. What is the Holy Spirit's role as we seek to apply Biblical wisdom? How do we avail ourselves of His help?

Chapter Eight

1. Do you struggle to understand the Bible? What is hard to understand? What has helped you understand?

2. Have you experienced others using a descriptive text as a prescriptive text?

3. How did Jesus explain our relationship with the Law before His death? How did Paul explain it afterwards?

Chapter Nine

1. What piece of wisdom from Proverbs 31 stands out to you?

2. What does it look like for you to be FOR those God has called you to help in your context?

3. What does it mean to you to be a safe place for your
    husband? How does this wisdom transcend marriage?

Chapter Ten

1. Have you experienced someone denying you love or
    honor until you met a certain standard in their minds?
    Have you experienced unconditional love or honor? How
    did you respond internally and externally to each?

2. How does Scripture link submission to Jesus?

3. What is the difference in showing unconditional love and
    enabling?

Chapter Eleven

1. Have you ever felt left out of discussions or studies on Biblical womanhood because of your life circumstances? Has this study helped or hurt you that way?

2. The Bible speaks of women in very different historical contexts. Women in the world today live in very different cultures and contexts. How does the Bible transcend culture or context to speak universal truth to women?

3. Do you have unfulfilled longing in your life for which you are waiting? What does enduring mean in your context?

4. How does the gospel equip you to stand firm and not fret as you wait for the fulfillment of all of God's promises to you?

CPSIA information can be obtained at www.ICGtesting.com
Printed in the USA
BVOW041023240413

319019BV00017B/248/P